HAUNTED
INDIAN RIVER
COUNTY

HAUNTED INDIAN RIVER COUNTY

LAWRENCE LAWSON

Haunted America

Published by Haunted America
A Division of The History Press
Charleston, SC
www.historypress.com

Copyright © 2024 by Lawrence Lawson
All rights reserved

First published 2024

Manufactured in the United States

ISBN 9781467155748

Library of Congress Control Number: 2023948362

CONTENTS

DEDICATION

This book is dedicated to my family for their support and patience not only in writing this book but also for the journey this quest has taken me on.

It is also dedicated to the wonderful people who live and work in Indian River County, Florida. Without their stories and knowledge, this book would not have been possible.

ACKNOWLEDGEMENTS

I would like to acknowledge and thank the following people and organizations that have been such an important part of this book.

Nikki Shrieves, for all the guidance she offered in completing this book.

Kelley Graham, for all her help in the development of this book.

James "Jim" Wilson, photographer extraordinaire, for his photographs that are found in the book and for his help in the collecting and review of many others.

Indian River County historian Ruth Stanbridge for her guidance and knowledge, which made all of this possible.

Ryan Lawson and Evan Lawson, my sons, who were an integral part of making all this possible. I love you, boys!

Charlotte and Mark Tripson for all their effort in unlocking the mystery and lore of the man who helped put Indian River County on the map: Waldo Sexton.

The Indian River County Historical Society, the Indian River Public Library and the team from Indian River Hauntings/Florida Bureau of Paranormal Investigations.

PREFACE

The world of paranormal investigation and research is filled with controversy. Unequivocal proof of the afterlife has eluded mankind since the beginning of time. Will what actually exists on the other side ever be revealed? Maybe not, but the quest to discover what happens after we leave this reality will continue.

The paranormal draws the interest of many different types of people. Some are believers in the paranormal, thirsting for more information. Some are unsure, looking for evidence to prove or disprove the existence of the other side. Others are just looking for a good scare. But one aspect that brings all readers of this genre together is the history. An often overlooked fact about paranormal research and investigation is that to be successful, you must love and understand the significance of history. Without a grasp of the past, none of the rest makes sense.

The history of Indian River County is rich and complicated. What has been chronicled in this book are not only the legends of this land but also some of the experiences of myself and my colleagues. This is really the reason for this book: to share what we have encountered and learned, as well as bring awareness to the rich history found in this part of Florida.

Whatever the reason you are joining me on this journey, searching for the ghosts of Indian River County is truly an adventure, and I hope you will enjoy learning more about this aspect of the famous Treasure Coast of Florida.

My name is Larry Lawson. I am a retired law enforcement officer and criminal justice educator. I am also a paranormal investigator and researcher. Unlike many who believe in the existence of ghosts, I did not have an experience of the paranormal in my childhood.

My first experience came not long after I began my career in law enforcement, in 1980, as a correctional officer in the Dade County Jail in Miami, Florida. It was the middle of a midnight watch when I observed the figure of a tall, thin man walking along the catwalk on the opposite side of a cell block. At first, I thought it was our lieutenant, who enjoyed coming up the stairs behind the control booth to check on the floor officers. But as quickly as I saw the figure, it vanished. I alerted the two other officers on the floor to what I saw. They checked the floor and the catwalk, only to reveal that there was no one else there. Expecting to be teased by my colleagues about seeing things, I was instead told that they were not surprised because they felt the jail was haunted.

While the incident never completely left my thoughts, time and life went on. I eventually became a police officer and, like many young rookies, spent most of my time on the midnight watch. Like everyone in the public safety field, I dealt with the ugliness and tragedy of society. I cannot speak for all cops, firefighters and paramedics, but there are quite a few of us who have encountered things we cannot explain. Is it because of what we do and when we are doing it? Our job puts us into situations the average person never experiences, such as answering a burglar alarm call at three o'clock in the morning only to find that the building is locked up tight and there's no indication of a problem. Was it the air-conditioning system coming on that caused a balloon or other object to set off the alarm? Was it a small creature that passed by the sensor, tripping the system? Then there are those times when you stop a car and something just says to you quietly in your mind, "Be careful on this one," and then you find out that the driver is wanted and he has a gun on him. Coincidence? Gut feeling? A guardian angel? Most of us just pass these things off until they become too obvious to ignore, and then you have to ask yourself if there is something on the other side warning you. Ask any law enforcement officer, firefighter, paramedic or nurse you know if they have had an experience. You might hear some very interesting stories.

This happened to me throughout my career. I often wondered who was out there watching over me. That question haunted me for years and ultimately drove me to research the paranormal. The journey began unexpectedly in 2009 when my oldest son, Ryan, asked me to take him to St. Augustine, Florida, on his eleventh birthday for a haunted tour of the lighthouse. What happened there changed my perspective on the afterlife and, in turn, the direction of my life. Ryan and I took the tour once and enjoyed it so much that we signed up for the next tour as well. The guide told us that since this new group was small, and Ryan and I had already gone through it once, he would allow us time in the lighthouse alone while he took the others to the lightkeeper's house. What an offer! We took advantage of the opportunity and sat quietly in one of the upper levels of the lighthouse, quietly listening. It was here that we had an experience that changed us profoundly.

According to history, when the lighthouse was being rebuilt, three little girls died in a tragic accident while playing on the construction site. It is said that they've continued to haunt the property since. Suddenly, both Ryan and I heard the unmistakable sound of children laughing. There was no question about what we were hearing. We were up high enough inside the lighthouse that there was no way it could be coming from the outside. The sound was clear and close by. I immediately began to look for speakers, wires or some logical reason for hearing the laughing. There was nothing. The laughter of these little girls came from somewhere I couldn't explain. The incident didn't frighten us. Instead, it led us on a quest that we still follow today, investigating paranormal phenomena and searching for the answers that have been eluding the world for generations: what exists on the other side of life as we know it.

The St. Augustine experience led to the creation of the Florida Bureau of Paranormal Investigation (FBPI), so named by my son Ryan in 2011. Over the ensuing years, more people wanted to know about what we found as we continued to investigate. Requests for tours and presentations on the phenomena led to the creation of Indian River Hauntings (now an outreach of the FBPI). We quickly became aware that many people expected to have the same experiences they saw on the television shows. However, the reality of paranormal investigations and research is not often "as seen on TV." Police work is the same way. Television and movies dramatize it and make it much more exciting than it usually is. I have had the pleasure of meeting several paranormal television personalities, and most of them are sincere and personable individuals. But television is for entertainment, and that's how it is structured. If you watched a paranormal show and nothing ever happened, would you still watch it every week?

I explain what paranormal investigations are really like in the same way I would describe police stakeouts as shown on television or in the movies. Those operations are filled with adrenaline-pumping excitement from the moment they begin. The reality of police stakeouts is that they are long and boring. You will wait for hours and might get thirty seconds of that adrenaline rush. Paranormal investigations are no different—that's the reality. Because of this, it has always been the philosophy of the FBPI and Indian River Hauntings to keep it real. From the beginning, the FBPI has been focused on finding evidence of the paranormal, collecting it, preserving it, analyzing it and using it to determine the existence of life after death. This has led to years of creating and refining protocols that help give us the ability to successfully capture and examine this evidence. Today, the FBPI continues to search for new ways to meet these goals. It is a seemingly never-ending task but one we willingly take on. As a team, we all share the same vision and goal: to discover the truth behind this paranormal phenomenon. We want people who are interested in what we do to understand our reality. Sometimes that means the investigation is absolutely boring, with no evidence collected. On the flip side, you have those moments when you do capture something and—eureka! That adrenaline rush comes, and it's all worthwhile.

I do not pretend to know what causes paranormal experiences. In my opinion, if anyone claims they actually know what it is and how it occurs, they are either fooling themselves or trying to fool you. I, like everyone else, have an opinion or belief about what it is. Is it the energy of spirits of those who have passed on before us? Different dimensions? Our own mind creating these events? I don't know for sure, but it is my goal to try to find that answer. I can tell you that, for generations, there have been stories from all cultures and walks of life about the paranormal. There must be some explanation for that. Thanks for joining me on this adventure.

INTRODUCTION

Florida is such an interesting state, so new yet so old. Claimed by Spain in the early 1500s by Juan Ponce de León, it was later the territory of Great Britain from 1763 to 1784. In 1784, it was returned to Spain and remained Spanish until it became a territory of the United States in 1821. Finally, in 1845, Florida became a state. While Florida had begun to experience growth by the 1850s, very little settlement occurred south of the Orlando/Kissimmee area. There were no roads or railways south of Orlando, and the east-central region of Florida did not begin to experience any substantial development until the 1880s. Despite the late expansion in Florida, the state lays claim to the oldest city in the continental United States: St. Augustine. But before the first Spanish adventurers were here, Indigenous peoples thrived in this subtropical paradise for more than a millennium. Those inhabitants of what we now call the Treasure Coast were known as the Ais and are considered by some to be one of the most sophisticated tribes that existed in ancient Florida. They were a part of Florida until the 1700s and lived in the area between Cape Canaveral and the southern end of present-day St. Lucie County, between the cities of Stuart and Port St. Lucie.

In July 1715, a fleet of Spanish treasure ships, known as the Spanish Plate Fleet, sank in a hurricane as it sailed line abreast off the coast of Florida from present-day Hobe Sound to present-day Sebastian. These twelve ships carried gold, jewels and other precious items that had been stolen from the peoples of Central and South America. The fleet was taking its ill-gotten gains back to the king of Spain for his treasury and to build a dowry for his daughter. All twelve ships sank, laden with their heavy cargo, when the storm struck, distributing these riches across the ocean floor right off the coast of present-day Martin, St. Lucie and Indian River Counties. These three counties would forever be known as the Treasure Coast of Florida. Despite the work of many treasure hunters throughout the years, including the famous Mel Fisher, some believe the treasure is still held captive by the sea.

When Florida became a state in 1842, most of its development occurred near seaports and waterways. On the Treasure Coast of Florida, there were encampments or settlements as early as the 1840s. For example, Fort Pierce, the town just south of Indian River County, was named for a fortification constructed by Brevet Lieutenant Colonel Benjamin K. Pierce, First U.S. Artillery, United States Army, in 1842. Lieutenant Colonel Pierce was the brother of the future fourteenth president of the United States, Benjamin Franklin Pierce. The fort was built to assist General Thomas Sidney Jesup in executing his battle plans during the Second Seminole War (1835–42). The site was abandoned a few years later and was burned to the ground in 1842. Interestingly enough, the area of what became Fort Pierce was originally an Ais Indian settlement and possibly the site of a 1500s-era Spanish mission. Today, it is open to the public as a park of the City of Fort Pierce on Indian River Drive, a short distance south of the St. Lucie County Courthouse.

The Civil War came and went without any significant development. While there were settlements in the areas of what are now known as Vero Beach and Sebastian in the mid-1800s, it wasn't until 1887 that a man named Henry Gifford opened the first mercantile store in the fledgling town of Vero. Gifford later applied for and opened the first post office in 1891, naming it Vero. Legend has it that Henry's wife, Sarah, used the Latin word *veritas*, meaning "truthfulness," from which the name Vero was derived. Thus, the town of Vero was formed. Both of Henry Gifford's buildings still stand today on the south side of Twentieth Street less than a block from US Highway 1.

But it was the City of Fellsmere that became the first incorporated municipality in present-day Indian River County. By 1905, Fellsmere had become the next largest city in the area after Fort Pierce. This is significant because when Fellsmere was incorporated in 1915, Indian River County was not yet established. Fellsmere, Vero and Sebastian were all part of the northern end of St. Lucie County. Vero followed suit and was incorporated in 1919 with Sebastian, becoming a municipality in 1924. In 1925, Vero was renamed Vero Beach and Indian River County was formed with Vero Beach as the county seat.

The 1920s brought Prohibition to this country, and the Treasure Coast was very much a part of it all. From moonshiners pumping out gallons of illegal alcohol to smugglers hauling in rum and other "spirits" from the Bahamas and Caribbean islands, Indian River County was a hotbed of activity. Bootleggers, smugglers and moonshine still operators found this part of Florida very inviting between the swamps, lagoons and uninhabited glades, not to mention the proximity to the British-ruled Bahamian Islands. The famous Ashley Gang, for example, was a crime family headed by John Ashley and his girlfriend Laura Upthegrove that excelled in moonshine still operations and importing illegal liquor from the Bahamas. Laura and John became a crime team years before Bonnie and Clyde began their crime wave. They brought Bahamian liquor and moonshine to speakeasies and bootleggers from Sebastian to Oslo in the southern part of present-day Indian River County, including the barrier islands where Vero Beach's beachside community exists today.

It was in northern present-day Indian River County (St. Lucie County at the time), at the bridge on the Old Dixie Highway crossing into Brevard County, that the Ashley Gang met their demise on November 1, 1924. Ashley and his three lieutenants (Ray Lynn, Clarence Middleton and Hanford Mobley) had decided to leave for Jacksonville for a while after a violent confrontation with the sheriff of Palm Beach County. They were to take the Old Dixie Highway (US Highway 1 was not in existence yet) to get there. The gang was confronted by St. Lucie County sheriff J.R. Merritt at the bridge that crossed over a fork in the Indian River. This meeting resulted in the death of Ashley and his men. But what became of Laura Upthegrove? She was reportedly angry over Ashley and his men going to Jacksonville without her and tipped off their movement to Palm Beach County sheriff Bob Baker. Baker called on his colleague, St. Lucie County sheriff Merritt, to intervene, which he did.

After the death of Ashley and the others, Laura moved to a community near Lake Okeechobee, where she later died under strange circumstances. The story of the Ashley Gang is deeply rooted in the history of the Treasure Coast, but it was here in Indian River County that it ended.

This wasn't the first death in the area that was connected to Prohibition. In 1920, St. Lucie County sheriff W.T. Jones died when the boat he was on, filled with illegal alcohol confiscated by his deputies, exploded. The boat was moored at the Oslo Boat ramp in present-day southern Indian River

County. Sheriff Jones boarded the vessel at the dock to sail it to the county seat in Fort Pierce. After leaving the dock, the boat mysteriously exploded, killing Jones.

But there is so much more to Indian River County than just bootleggers and smugglers. There was Waldo Sexton, the man many credit with shining a light on the beauty of the area for the rest of the world. The Los Angeles Dodgers (formerly the Brooklyn Dodgers) made their spring training home in Vero Beach in 1947. Indian River County was also world-renowned for "Indian River Citrus," the pride of the Florida citrus industry for decades.

This quiet, relaxing coastal community hidden from the rest of world by water, swamps and reefs became known as the hidden jewel of Florida. Often, Vero Beach was referred to as the gateway to the tropics. Unbeknownst to many is the dark side of this hidden treasure.

All these changes came with colorful events and stories that became legends. Some of these legends included stories of the afterlife. Many of the souls named in these tales are said to still roam the streets, parks and buildings of Indian River County.

In the following chapters, we'll focus on three cities in Indian River County: Vero Beach, Sebastian/Roseland and Fellsmere. Discover their rich histories—but most importantly, their haunted past!

PART I
VERO BEACH: A HISTORY

This quiet oceanside community was, and in many ways still is, a hidden gem on the south/central east coast of the state of Florida. Vero Beach is divided by the majestic Indian River, an intercoastal waterway that has existed since long before the area was inhabited. On the mainland, you find much of the residential, business and governmental areas of the city. Across the Indian River, you find the barrier island that extends north into Brevard County and into St. Lucie County to the south. Here, residents and visitors enjoy the true riches of coastal life in Florida: quaint shops, wonderful restaurants, hotels and much more—but most of all, the relaxed lifestyle that allows one to shed the stresses of daily life in today's world.

In days long past, this was the home of the Ais Indians, considered by many to be one of the prominent tribes in the precolonial days of the Sunshine State. The Ais were not farmers but hunter-gatherers who were recognized for their hunting and fishing prowess. Their land covered most of the coastal area from today's Cape Canaveral to approximately the Martin and St. Lucie county line between Stuart and Port St. Lucie. They inhabited land as far west as Fellsmere and slightly beyond. One of their largest villages was known as Jece. While the exact location of this village is still open for debate, many believe that it sat on what is locally known today as the Rio Mar Country Club, an exclusive community on the sandy beaches of the barrier island. As time passed, Europeans, specifically the Spanish, arrived in the area and ushered in a new era. The Ais and other tribes, such as the Jeaga, who inhabited the area just south of the Ais, passed into oblivion thanks to war, disease and the encroachment of Europeans. The Ais were gone by the 1740s.

Vero was established in 1919 by several individuals who pioneered the area. Names such as Graves, Zeuch, Reems and Sexton—just to name a few—helped build the community. It was a man named Henry Gifford who gave a name to this budding town, later touted to be "Where the Tropics Begin." Henry Gifford was an early merchant in town and, in 1891, opened the first post office, with Henry as its first postmaster.

As the area was developed, generally under the auspices of the Indian River Farms Corporation, plans were made to drain the swampy areas for inhabitation, planting of crops and caring for cattle. Canals were dug throughout the area to deal with the wet terrain as well as handle the subtropical rain common to the area. One of these canals, which runs next to Vero Beach's current airport, produced key evidence of inhabitation of the area around 1914. The remains of prehistoric animals such as mastodons, woolly mammoths and saber-toothed tigers were uncovered. The remains of ancient humans were also found. These remains were dated earlier than most human inhabitants of North America and immediately put Vero Beach on the archaeological map.

Through the Roaring Twenties, this tiny, largely unknown paradise began to develop. US Highway 1 was completed in the late 1920s. The Great Depression followed the 1929 crash of the stock market, bringing hardship to those who lived here. World War II came in 1941. This time of war also brought development to the area, as Naval Air Station Vero Beach sprang up from the groves and pastures of the area to help train U.S. Navy and Marine Corps aircrews for combat against the Axis powers. After the war, prosperity grew in Indian River County. Not only did the Brooklyn Dodgers travel south to Vero Beach to conduct their spring training, but the famous Piper Aircraft Corporation built its headquarters in Vero as well. Vero Beach was finally coming of age.

Vero is still a destination for many to vacation and enjoy the warm sun during the cold winter months up north. Indian River County offers a place for people to forget about the troubles of everyday life. It also offers an interesting glimpse into the past, sometimes through the eyes of those who lived here long before us.

CHAPTER 1

SEXTON / TRIPSON HOMESTEAD

T he home that Waldo Sexton built for himself and his wife, Elsbeth, in 1914 is located on the north side of Twelfth Street, between Forty-Third and Fifty-Eighth Avenues, in Vero Beach. The property is now known as Waldo's Secret Garden, in honor of the man that put Vero Beach on the map. Waldo came to Vero around 1913 from the state of Indiana to sell farm equipment. He fell in love with the beautiful seaside town and never left, becoming its most famous citizen and entrepreneur. Known as the consummate salesman, Waldo Sexton sold Vero Beach to the world, creating or co-creating places such as the Patio Restaurant, McKee Jungle Garden (built with Arthur McKee), Waldo's Mountain and the Driftwood Resort. He became an independent citrus grower and a cattleman. Waldo Sexton even developed three varieties of avocado, one of which bears his name.

The residence was originally a single-story dwelling that developed into a two-story home in which Waldo raised his family. In 1924, the property also became the site of the first commercial dairy in the area, bearing the name Vero Beach Dairy. It later became known as the Tripson Dairy when Waldo passed the operation over to his new son-in-law, John Tripson, who had married Waldo's daughter Barbara. Waldo built a home for Barbara and John just a few yards west of his residence. It was from here that the Tripsons operated the dairy until 1981. Today, Waldo's rustic home is still occupied by Sexton/Tripson descendants—as well as, it seems, by Waldo himself. The property is now used for special events, particularly weddings,

Waldo Sexton's home in Vero Beach, Florida. Built in 1914, it was Waldo's home until he died in 1957. It remains in the Sexton family. *Jim Wilson Photography.*

and the house built for John and Barbara is a guesthouse. Its timeless and rustic beauty brings visitors back to a bygone era and perhaps allows its more permanent guests to be in more familiar surroundings.

The history of Waldo's homestead is as legendary and rich as its paranormal history. Reports include doors opening on their own and footsteps heard where no one was present. Shadows and full-body apparitions have also been widely reported. Guests and family members have described hearing voices and strange noises, lights coming on and off by themselves and water faucets turning on without anyone present. These episodes occur in both Waldo's and the Tripsons' home. Others have also reported seeing the apparition of John Tripson inside the Tripson residence years after his passing. Hildie Tripson, wife of Waldo's grandson Mark Tripson, told of one incident. When Hildie's son was a child, he was in the Tripson house and saw a man standing there whom he did not recognize. The figure looked at the young Tripson boy and said, "I'm Waldo. Who are you?" When Hildie's son told his parents about the encounter, his description of the unknown man matched Waldo Sexton exactly—a man he had never met in person. Hildie Tripson, who passed away in April 2021, spoke of many unexplained episodes in the two homes on the property, along with the surrounding grounds. But perhaps the most intriguing experience of all was her possible return from the other side.

At the request of Mark and Hildie Tripson, paranormal investigators were invited to do research on the property and were greeted with a wide array of evidence, including unexplained voices, inexplicable energy spikes, doors slamming closed and other strange anomalies caught on their equipment.

During one paranormal investigation, a voice was captured inside Waldo's home saying the name Louise. Unknown to the investigators at the time, Louise was the name of Waldo's mother-in-law, who passed away in the home during the 1960s.

Investigations inside the Tripson home have made several investigators ill, forcing them to leave. On another occasion, investigators made contact with an entity in the kitchen who claimed to be Waldo's daughter, Barbara Tripson. With the aid of dowsing rods used by the investigators, Barbara made it clear that she did not like to cook and preferred to be playing tennis!

Investigations have also ventured to the property outside of the homes, including much of the old dairy property. Areas that had no source of electricity near them began to suddenly produce very high EMF (electronic magnetic field) readings that would suddenly disappear for no apparent reason. Batteries that were fresh or recently recharged rapidly drained. The slamming of a heavy door inside the diary bottling plant was heard by investigators. When the team investigated visually, they found that there were no doors in the building that would have made that sound.

Several times, the name Eddie was heard on listening and recording devices. It was later found that Eddie was the name of Waldo Sexton's right-hand man in the 1920s and 1930s. It is alleged that Eddie, in fit of rage, killed a man at another location after discovering that the man had been having a romantic relationship with Eddie's wife. Eddie allegedly hid the murder weapon on the Sexton property. He was never charged with the killing.

Another compelling piece of evidence from the property was the appearance of a figure on a type of specialized camera known as a structured light sensor (SLS) camera. The investigators were in a grassy area between the main house and the back portion of the property. With the camera, they viewed a figure sitting in a vacant chair. The figure stayed for several minutes, even crossing its legs as if earnestly listening to the conversation. Then, as suddenly as it appeared, it vanished.

But in August 2021, four months after the passing of Hildie, the investigative team was called back. This time, they were accompanied by

The Tripson home. This was the home of Waldo Sexton's daughter Barbara and her husband, John Tripson. It is located next to Waldo's residence. *Jim Wilson Photography.*

Sitting area underneath the Tripson home next to the Flower Room. *Jim Wilson Photography.*

medium Chris Huff from Durham, England. Chris Huff is an internationally known medium and psychic who regularly lends his expertise during investigations with the team brought in by the Tripson family. Following the usual protocol for these investigations, Chris joined via the Internet and was not provided any information about where the team was or the history of the location. This allows for any information he can provide to be free of contamination by having knowledge of the venue. During the walk-through, Chris was left on video call in a place known as the Flower Room. The Flower Room lies underneath the main floor of the Tripson house, which is elevated by stilts, leaving a large space directly underneath the main house. As Chris was left to view the Flower Room through the Internet, he experienced something he could not explain. He said that out of nowhere, the wispy, opaque face of a woman appeared on the screen. This was followed by a casket appearing in the room. Chris said the screen then went black. When contact was reestablished with Chris, he explained what occurred to the investigator. He stated that the appearance of the casket was an indication of a death. Unknown to the investigative team at the time, and certainly unknown to Chris Huff, this was the same room where Hildie Tripson suddenly passed away just a few months earlier. Was this Hildie Tripson retuning to let her family and friends know that she was still home? Was she confirming that there is something after this existence? Only time, and maybe another visit from Hildie, will tell.

So, is the homestead of one of Vero Beach's most famous personalities haunted? One only needs to visit the grounds to find out. Anyone who does cannot help but feel that they have traveled back to a simpler time. The events experienced by family members, guests and investigators at the Sexton homestead give an even deeper connection with the past. This connection is a bridge to the other side, where those who walked the property in years past are still very much a part of its fabric today.

CHAPTER 2

THE BEACH AREA

The ocean side of the barrier island in Indian River County boasts some of the most beautiful and serene beaches in Florida. Visitors travel from all over the state, the country and even from abroad to enjoy what the area has to offer. However, the areas with the most paranormal interest are the beach, the Ocean Grill, Waldo's Mountain and the historical local landmark known as the the Driftwood Resort. These beaches have not always been a place for families and vacationers to visit. In the early days of the east-central coast of Florida, shipwrecks along the reefs near shore took the lives of many—the most famous being the twelve-ship Spanish Plate Fleet carrying stolen treasures from Central America to Spain in 1715. When they were lashed by a hurricane in late July that year, all ships of the fleet were line abreast from roughly Hobe Sound to Sebastian. The vast amount of treasure that was lost in this disaster is what gave the coastline of Indian River, St. Lucie and Martin Counties the title the "Treasure Coast." The area became so well known for seaborne disasters that the federal government set up a series of shelters, known as Houses of Refuge, designed to render aid to stranded sailors and passengers who were marooned in this subtropical land.

Stories of pirates and treasure hunters scouring the barrier islands for the lost treasures of the Spanish Plate Fleet are numerous. But lost are the other shipwrecks and sinkings that have occurred along this coast. Seafarers faced the threat of death from not only the sea but also the Indigenous population inhabiting the coastline.

Vero's beachside. *Jim Wilson Photography.*

In 1696, young Jonathan Dickinson, the son of a wealthy merchant in Port Royal, Jamaica, was traveling to a new city in the new world, a place called Philadelphia. He set sail on August 23, 1696, during the height of hurricane season in the Caribbean. On September 22, 1696, Dickinson—aboard one of his family's ships, the *Reformation*—was hit by a strong storm as it traveled off the coast of Florida near present-day Stuart. The *Reformation* was thrown into the reef, where it was severely damaged and beached. As the sun came up the next day, the survivors were met by a band of Natives who became aggressive and threatened the lives of the survivors. It was only by chance that these Indigenous people, possibly the Jeaga people, decided not to do them harm but instead take them as prisoners back to their village. The Jeaga warriors stripped them of their clothing and belongings, including the supplies salvaged from the *Reformation*. The Dickinson party stayed as the unwelcome guests of the Jeaga until they were taken to the village of Jece, one of the largest villages of the Ais Nation and the Jeagas' neighbors to the north. The Ais were said to have a deal with the Spaniards, with whom they had established a trade partnership. The deal was to take shipwreck survivors and turn them over to the Spanish for a reward. The Jeagas were likely aware of this deal, so they made an exchange.

The village of Jece was on the barrier island of present-day Indian River County, and it was here that the Dickinson party, including Dickinson, his wife and their infant son, spent the next two months before some members

Figure caught on the beach not far from the Driftwood Resort. *Jim Wilson Photography*.

of the party were taken to St. Augustine by Spanish traders. Dickinson made it to St. Augustine and eventually to Philadelphia, where he later became mayor. It was here that he penned his book, taken from the journal he had been keeping throughout his journey to the New World. This book, *Jonathan Dickenson's Journal*, became the only detailed written account of the Ais tribe.

The rest of the castaways, however, were to get to St. Augustine by foot or other means. It was on their trek that the rest of the group, who were underfed, underclothed and in poor health, perished on the beaches in today's Indian River County.

This was only the beginning of the tragedies that would occur on these shores, and these tragedies bring weight to the stories and reports of hauntings in the area. One story tells of an occurrence on April 30, 1894. On this date, the SS *Breconshire*, a passenger/cargo vessel, ran aground near the present-day Driftwood Resort. The ship went down on the reefs in approximately thirty feet of water. A rescue crew from the House of Refuge, approximately one mile away near Bethel Creek, sprang into action. The rescue crew got to the sinking vessel in time to save all hands aboard the *Breconshire*. But on their arrival back to the House of Refuge, they began to hear cries for help coming from the ocean. The rescuers confirmed that all passengers and crew of the *Breconshire* were accounted for, but still the voices could be heard. The crew went back to the scene of the sinking and found no one. There was no explanation for what they heard, and to this day, the mystery has never been solved.

Many have heard these sorrowful cries for help along the beaches of Indian River County and have called local law enforcement to assist. Testimony from dispatchers has confirmed that these calls still occur today.

A local professional photographer, Jim Wilson, has confirmed his own experiences on these beaches. He has heard cries for help from the beach and found nothing. Jim is well known as a local authority on the 1715 Spanish Plate Fleet disaster and has taken a series of photographs at different spots on Vero's beaches that cannot be explained or debunked. These photographs depict figures on the beach when no living beings were around. One of these photographs was part of a series taken at the base of the stairs leading from the Driftwood Resort onto the beach. Of all the photographs Jim took in this set, only one showed a shadowy figure. This photo has been featured in a local magazine and has been the subject of local radio and newspaper interviews. It depicts a figure with a distinct but transparent human form. Many who have examined the photo believe the figure to be a Spanish sailor (due to the enlarged area on the chest that suggests a sailor's uniform).

However, paranormal researcher and medium Christopher Huff saw something else. Chris is world-renowned for his paranormal work, specifically in haunted airfields in the United Kingdom. When examining the photograph, he suggested that the enlarged area on the figure's chest is not part of a Spanish sailor's uniform but of a pilot's life jacket, commonly

Ghostly figure captured on the beach next to the base of the stairs leading into the Driftwood Resort. *Jim Wilson Photography*.

referred to during the years of World War II as a "Mae West," named after the well-known actress of the 1930s. He also noted a possible pilot's leather flying helmet being worn by the figure. The most telling part of his theory is a large anomaly seen on the leg of the figure. This spot corresponds to the location of a leg pocket often found on a pilot's flight suit used to hold maps or other necessities.

Vero Beach was the location of Naval Air Station (NAS) Vero Beach. NAS Vero Beach was a training site for U.S. Navy and Marine Corps aircrews. Whether the photograph was of a Spanish sailor dying in the storms of 1715 or a young American pilot killed while training to defend his country, this picture is a stark reminder of the tragic past on the shores of Indian River County. The sea has been the home of many stories of ghosts and hauntings throughout history. The shores of Indian River County are certainly no stranger to these events.

CHAPTER 3

THE OCEAN GRILL

Sitting out over the beach just north of the Driftwood Resort, the Ocean Grill was another creation of Waldo Sexton. Originally, it was not much more than a hot dog and hamburger stand built by Waldo to serve those who were enjoying the beachside spot he created for people to gather and visit. This area was later officially christened Sexton Plaza by the City of Vero Beach, as the citizens were grateful for all he had done for the town. As time wore on, he sold the restaurant destined to be called the Ocean Grill to the Adler family, around the time of World War II. Because the Adlers' last name had German origins, it is said that many in the community refused to patronize the restaurant and business declined. As the story goes, the Adlers disappeared without anyone's knowledge. Did they leave town? Were they whisked away by the U.S. government as spies? Did they take a boat or raft and paddle out to the Nazi submarines known as U-boats that lurked off the coast of Vero Beach looking for Allied shipping heading toward Europe? This was certainly a possibility, as the coastal area had been the hunting grounds for German U-boats, which had already sunk several ships along the coast. Just south of NAS Vero Beach, in Fort Pierce, was another naval training area (the birthplace and home of the U.S. Navy "frogman" program, later to be known as the Navy SEALS), and these sites certainly would have attracted attention from the Axis powers.

Whatever the reason may be, the Adlers left, and Waldo regained ownership of the restaurant and expanded it as a place for military personnel and local citizens to come and enjoy the beachside amenities. Interestingly,

The Ocean Grill Restaurant on Vero's Beach. *Larry Lawson.*

Waldo built an outdoor dance floor connected to the restaurant so that those visiting the establishment could dance under the stars. This dance floor opened, and diners danced outside for one night. The guests who were enjoying the moonlight dance were suddenly attacked by a well-known pest in Florida. This pest, locally known as a no-see-um, is a tiny, gnat-like insect that inflicts an irritating, and at times painful, bite. Their name originated because you can't see them until you become one of their victims. Because of these annoying pests, Waldo immediately decided to close the dance floor and put up walls and a roof. Today it is the main dining area inside the Ocean Grill Restaurant.

The restaurant was a favorite hangout for Waldo Sexton. It includes a large mahogany table that was said to be originally owned by a past president of the Philippines. A section of the restaurant known as the Blood Room, not named for any nefarious reason, was said to be a favorite room of Waldo's that he is believed to still frequent to this day.

This well-known and upscale restaurant on Vero's Beach has long been a favorite dining spot for locals and tourists alike. However, there are rumors that Waldo still enjoys hanging around one of his favorite haunts. On occasion, he has reportedly been seen inside the restaurant—undoubtedly making sure all is in order.

CHAPTER 4

WALDO'S MOUNTAIN

Waldo Sexton built and developed things that would not only bring notoriety to Vero Beach but also ensure a profit. Yet one place that he built was simply to attract visitors. It is said that this spot was the only tourist attraction he ever built that was not designed to make a profit but simply as a place to enjoy. This was known as Waldo's Mountain.

Waldo's Mountain was created as the result of the dredging occurring to develop an area that is as known as Bethel Creek. This land was on the barrier island nestled between the Indian River and the ocean just west of present-day Highway A1A. This property was owned by Waldo Sexton and is just north of the site of the current Bethel Creek House community building, which is owned by the City of Vero Beach.

Waldo asked the dredging crews to pile up the spoils of their work onto adjacent land that he owned. They agreed and left more than forty feet of dredging spoils behind. When Waldo returned several days later and saw the massive amount of dirt, he created his latest vision to date. Some have claimed he wanted to create the tallest point in this part of the state—and perhaps in all of Florida. He molded the pile into Waldo's Mountain and topped it off with a tall piece of lumber. He then proceeded to decorate the mountain with steps made of painted ceramic tiles and other unusual artifacts before proclaiming its creation to the world. What was known by some of the old-time residents of Vero Beach was that the spot was also the location of an ancient and sacred Ais Indian burial site. The Ais, who inhabited this area until the early 1700s, held a deep spiritual connection to

Waldo Sexton sitting on the steps of Waldo's Mountain surrounded by the Dolphinettes swim team. *Sexton Photo Collection via Charolette Tripson.*

the land. It has been said that human remains were found in the spoils used to build the mountain, including an Ais skull. It is believed by some that the grounds were and are cursed for having been disturbed.

The mountain sat there for years, and it was Waldo's wish that he be buried there. This, unfortunately, would not be the case. When Waldo passed away in 1967, he was buried in the family plot in the City of Vero Beach's cemetery. Many suggested that the refusal to abide by his wishes would anger his spirit. Some argue that it did just that.

It was probably good fortune that Waldo's family made the decision not to bury him on the mountain, because in 1972, a severe storm ripped through the area. The erosion caused by the storm threatened to take both Waldo's beloved Driftwood Resort and the Ocean Grill restaurant into the Atlantic Ocean. It was decided that the now decaying remnants of the mountain would be used to shore up both buildings and save them from destruction. This included the alleged skull that was contained within the mountain. Could this be another one of the reasons that Waldo is known to still visit the Driftwood and the Ocean Grill?

In the early 1970s, the property was put up for sale. Several of the investors who attempted to buy the property for development were met with disaster. One met unexpected financial ruin. Another died from a sudden heart attack. Other prospective owners died in a plane crash and, allegedly, by suicide. Finally, one builder successfully purchased the property. This investor had heard the stories of the Ais burial mound, Waldo's Mountain and the possible curse left on the property. It was decided to construct the new building in a way that would honor Waldo. The new building, which would contain offices and a restaurant, would be made from wood and not modern building materials. This was done in the belief that it would appease the Ais, Waldo Sexton or whatever spirits inhabited the area. The south end of the building was pointed as if it was the bow of a ship. It was at this spot that Waldo's Mountain and its ancient contents once sat.

This is also the location of the restaurant that was to occupy the building. The restaurant was called the Ruddy Duck. The owner of this restaurant spoke of strange happenings inside the establishment. After the completion of the restaurant, there were claims of equipment unexplainably not working, dishes moving, drinking glasses breaking, doors opening and even sightings of Waldo himself. The owner, after contemplating the situation, understood that Waldo wanted to be recognized for his accomplishments in the development of Vero Beach. A picture of Waldo was put up in the restaurant for those who entered to see. It was even said that the owner requested that the staff tell Waldo, "Hello," when they entered and say, "Goodbye," and thank you for all he did when they left. Did this appease Waldo? Did it appease the spirits of the Ais? Will the land ever be at peace? Only time, and maybe Waldo Sexton, will tell.

CHAPTER 5
THE DRIFTWOOD RESORT

One of Waldo's most famous buildings went under construction in 1933. This was to be a weekend beach house for his family, located in a picturesque oceanfront setting. He chose to create a private beach house with a vintage look by using building material from destroyed buildings, actual driftwood and artifacts found from all over Florida. After he had the main house built, which included an approximately twenty-five-foot breezeway between two sections with living quarters above it, he expanded it to house more guests. Soon after its completion, Waldo decided that his new creation might do well as a beachside hotel, and the Driftwood Resort was born. In 1937, the Driftwood Resort began to welcome guests to the wonders of Vero's beachside. The Driftwood became the crown jewel of Waldo's accomplishments in Vero as visitors from around the world came to enjoy the beauty of Florida's Treasure Coast.

In 1967, Waldo Sexton passed away. He left a rich and colorful legacy for others to remember him and his accomplishments. Some say, however, that Waldo never really left. Reports of him being seen at the Driftwood long after his death are plentiful. Both resort staff and visitors have made mention of the eccentric "King of Vero Beach" returning to look over his kingdom from time to time. These reports include televisions in multiple locations mysteriously turning on, doorknobs being turned and doors being opened when there was nobody else around. Other guests have been woken overnight by unexplained sounds, with some describing words, music or noises by someone or something from a bygone era that shouldn't have been there.

Above: The famous Driftwood Resort on Vero's beachside. *Larry Lawson.*

Left: Waldo Sexton overlooking the Atlantic Ocean from his perch at the Driftwood Resort. *Sexton Photo Collection via Charlotte Tripson.*

Back in 2004, the entire Treasure Coast was ravaged by two hurricanes, Jeanne and Frances, within a one-week period. The entire area suffered serious damage, and the barrier island in Indian River County was closed off due to safety concerns. To secure the Driftwood Resort property and prevent any more damage, the late Ralph Sexton, son of Waldo Sexton, hired a crew to be helicoptered onto the property to begin a damage assessment and repairs. The crew consisted three workers and a supervisor. Within days of arrival, the supervisor contacted Ralph and asked a simple question: "Is the resort haunted?" Ralph Sexton chuckled and inquired why he was asking. The supervisor told Ralph that in addition to him and his crew, there was another "person" who kept going between the rooms, opening and closing doors and making a nuisance of themselves. The foreman went on to say that he and his crew were the only ones on the property.

Many stories come from the people who spend the most time on the property: the staff. While the resort employed the usual cleaning and maintenance staff, larger repair jobs were dealt with by repair specialists on retainer. It was in the spring of 2019 when some floor work needed to be done to the room that Waldo Sexton used when he stayed at the resort. This was the perfect day to do the work, because the room was not occupied, so the resort scheduled a workman to work on the floor. On his arrival, he checked in with the front office, got the key and headed toward Waldo's room. Soon thereafter, the radio at the front desk crackled and the voice of the workman came over the radio. The front office staff heard him say, "I thought you said there wasn't anyone in this room?" When the front desk clerk responded, saying, "There isn't anyone staying there," the workman simply replied, "Then who am I looking at?" The workman went on to describe a man that fit the description of Waldo Sexton. When other staff arrived at the room, no one was there.

In late 2021, a guest in one of the newer buildings at the resort complained of an incident that caused her to ask to be switched to another room. The guest told the front desk clerk, Joe Kelly, that a garbage can moved on its own from one spot to another and it frightened her so much that she demanded to be given another room. What the guest didn't know was that Waldo's wife, Elsbeth, had lived in that building until her death in 1986. This wasn't the only incident that Joe experienced. He has spoken of televisions being on in rooms where no one was registered. He has even described how the television in the reception room next to the check-in desk would turn on by itself—at the same time every night.

Stories like this are plentiful. A number of years ago, a woman visiting with her twelve-year-old son, in the original resort building, woke up in the middle of the night to see a ghostly vision of a person standing at the foot their bed. Her description of that apparition was of Waldo Sexton. Some people have seen Waldo's apparition sitting in the Adirondack chairs lining the walks outside of hotel rooms. These figures were recognized to be Waldo based on the historical pictures and documents located in the resort.

One staff member, front desk manager Zach Zebrowski, tells an interesting story of an event that took place a few years earlier when he held a security position on the property. Staff and others observed a young lady on the beach near the stairs that led up to the resort. She was seen having a conversation with an unseen person. Those who watched her noted that while she looked young, her dress was reminiscent of what a hippie from the 1960s would wear. The people observing this event, including Zach, simply believed that this person may have had other issues causing her to speak to an invisible person. Keep in mind, this event occurred prior to the regular use of Bluetooth devices. A short time later, Zach received a call that there was an unregistered guest who somehow was able to get into one of the rooms, the room where Waldo himself used to stay, without checking in. Zach then went to the room and knocked on the door. To his surprise, he was greeted by the young "hippie" woman he had seen earlier on the beach. He asked the young lady how she gained entrance to the room. Apparently, an unwitting resort employee had unlocked the door of the room for her. But when she was asked how she chose that room, she simply said that the man on the beach said it was his room and gave her permission. She was told that no one was registered in the room, but she insisted that the man on the beach said it was alright. When she was asked who this man was, she provided a physical description of Sexton and said that his name was Waldo.

Had Waldo Sexton returned on these occasions to visit his property to check on it? Had he taken a liking to this young lady dressed in clothing familiar to him?

In another incident that involved both the resort and its adjoining beach, paranormal investigators had rented the room Waldo Sexton stayed in. After some successful contact in the room, it was decided to investigate the beach. In an area where there was no man-made electrical interference that could have influenced the equipment, the readings were off the charts. It was as if there was something standing all around the investigators. During this investigation, one of the investigators broadcast live on social media that they were conducting an investigation. The investigator soon received a message from a person who claimed they had seen something they couldn't explain at the same spot on the beach the night before. They stated that they saw a figure standing there in the surf that suddenly disappeared. While the investigator was skeptical of the claim, historical inquiries revealed that same type of sighting had been experienced by others over the years. The photographs taken by Jim Wilson, as described earlier, were taken in this very same area. Could these be victims of the 1715 disaster or perhaps other victims of local shipwrecks over the centuries?

Waldo Sexton. *Sexton Photo Collection via Charlotte Tripson.*

At the Driftwood Resort, public tours are offered to share historical facts and ghostly legends of the area with those interested. Because of the nature of these tours, paranormal evidence is often revealed.

During one of these tours, a group visiting from Canada had an experience of their own. These guests were staying in one of the rooms in the original resort building. They had gone out for dinner, returning sometime later. When they opened the door, they could hear water running in the bathroom and went to investigate. When the guests got to the bathroom, they observed both the hot and cold faucets on full, the rubber stopper in the drain and the water about to pour over the sides of the tub. The husband then spoke up, saying, "And the hotel's hairdryer was in the middle of the tub—and when we left, it was on the counter, twenty feet away!" This is not the only report from this room. A few years earlier, another guest woke up to find what they described as an ancient Spanish sailor standing at the foot of their bed.

Other sightings have been reported as well. One member of the tour company stated that they have observed an apparition sitting on one of the chairs on the resort walkways. He saw a man in a striped shirt sitting on a chair. On closer inspection, the figure had no solid form, and just as quickly as he was seen, he vanished.

More recently, after completing a tour, several guests went down to the beach to try out some of the paranormal equipment offered for use during the event. As the tour guide waited for them in the breezeway of the original building, he suddenly heard a woman weeping loudly from behind him. He turned to see what the problem was, but there was no one there. He then checked the area for someone in distress, only to find that he was the only one there. A few weeks later, after another private tour had just concluded, the couple on this tour asked if the guide could take a few minutes to investigate the room they were staying in at the resort. They told him they felt there was activity in their room, describing how they woke up the night before hearing loud noises in the kitchen area. They went to investigate and found the doors of the room's kitchen cabinets opening and slamming shut—on their own!

Due to the ever-increasing sightings and experiences at the Driftwood Resort, there is little doubt that Waldo and maybe a few of his friends continue to enjoy the hospitality found there. If you have the opportunity to visit Vero Beach, you might want to consider a stay at the Driftwood Resort. If you do, you just might get a chance to meet the original owner.

CHAPTER 6
JUSTIN'S OF VERO

The property along the beach was not developed quickly. Most of the buildings you see there today were built in the 1960s, '70s and '80s. There was even more development as the twenty-first century approached. It wasn't until after World War II ended that Vero Beach began to grow into the town it is today. For example, as previously mentioned, the Brooklyn Dodgers major league baseball club selected Vero Beach as their new home for spring training. This momentous event was just one of the catalysts that brought the area into the national spotlight.

With Vero's tranquil and beautiful beaches, even more people began to make Indian River County their vacation destination. The beach began to grow with visitors and businesses. In the 1960s, a narrow building was built on property located on Ocean Drive, across the street and to the north of the Driftwood Resort. The top floor of this address is an upscale beachside hair salon known as Justin's of Vero. Next to this is another store known as Twig Swim and Sportswear. There is a walkway between these two buildings where visitors have reported strange activity. These sightings are of men carrying crates of alcohol from the doors of one building to the next along this walkway. Despite this, there are no doors in that walkway. Visitors have also seen strange lights that manifest from seemingly nowhere and just as suddenly disappear into one of the structures. Could these be the souls of the Spanish fleet or perhaps the notorious Ashley Gang that smuggled liquor through the area during Prohibition?

Entrance to Justin's Hair Salon on Vero's beachside. *Larry Lawson.*

The salon, owned by Justin Barnett, has also been the scene of numerous unexplained incidents experienced by both Justin and his staff.

Jolene Grant is one of the stylists in the shop. She has experienced hearing unexplained noises and knocks in the shop, as well as doors and windows opening and closing. She, like the owner, believes that the spirit of a women shares the salon space with her. But it was the owner, Justin Barnett, who described an event that convinced him of the presence of another entity in the salon. While he was working with a client, he leaned her back into the shampooing sink as he went to answer a phone call. When he returned, he found the water running in the sink. Not wanting to actually get the client's hair wet, he asked her if she had turned the water on. It was then that he noticed the wide-eyed look on his client's face. She responded to him that she did not touch the faucet in the sink, that it had turned on all by itself. Justin states that this was just one of the unexplained events that has occurred in the shop.

Members of the historical ghost tour company that conducts events throughout these grounds are often told new bits of paranormal experiences and historical tidbits by their guests, business owners and other visitors. In fact, it was Justin Barrett of the salon who approached the tour one evening asking if they were there to "investigate the lady" in his shop. This led to

Front desk of Justin's Hair Salon. *Larry Lawson.*

several investigations that confirmed much of what he and his staff had been experiencing. This chance meeting is what led to the investigation of Justin's of Vero by paranormal investigators.

During the first investigation, several pieces of interesting information were found. The most compelling of these happened during an electronic voice phenomenon (EVP) session using a voice recorder. During the session, the investigators asked, "Do you like what they have done to the building?" In response, a very clear female voice was heard saying, "Oh no!" on the recorder. It was later discovered that the original owner of the property wanted that narrow stretch of land unbuilt, keeping it a green area. After the property changed hands in the 1960s, the new owners built on it, against the wishes of the original owner. So the question "Do you like what they have done with building?" and the answer "Oh no!" take on an entirely new meaning.

Another story coming from this location was of a woman watching the tours from the western window of the salon. Seen by a tour staff member, she was described as having long dark hair and wearing a long white dress. The staff member said she was reaching out to him but he was unable to understand what she was trying to say. He did feel that she was quite sad.

During another beachside tour, two teenage girls were part of the group. During a stop next to Justin's of Vero, the two young ladies on the tour stopped the tour guide. One of them told the tour guide, "My friend has something to tell you." She told the guide how she saw someone in the western window of the salon. This was the same window in which the tour staff member had seen the women. The young lady described a woman in a long white dress with long dark hair. She said the woman was very sad. This description was the same as the one given by the tour staff member. This earlier experience had never been shared with another tour, yet this guest described exactly what the staff member had seen at an earlier time.

During a later investigation by the paranormal team, medium Christopher Huff was present via the Internet as a way to bridge the gap between the physical and spiritual planes of existence. Chris was not informed of the location of the investigation or any of the previous experiences of staff or guests. Chris was able to make a connection with a young woman who fit the description of the woman the staff member and the tour guest encountered. Not only was his description of the mysterious woman exactly the same, but he also noted her extreme sadness. Chris was able to say he believed the spirit's sadness was due to the loss of a child. What that loss entailed, he wasn't able to identify, but the pain she felt was clear and real to him. So, is this connection with a sad lady in white, seen by three different people at three different times, confirmation of her existence, or is it just coincidence?

At first, it was assumed that this spirit might be the same entity that was moving items and opening doors and windows in the salon. But after further investigation, it was believed that there was another entity present. Chris connected with a different spirit that appeared to him to be a very gregarious women who enjoyed interacting with the living. He described her as similar to the onstage personality of the 1930s film star Mae West. This was the woman responsible for the activity around the shop. While Chris did not have information about what type of activity occurred in the salon prior to this investigation, he was able to confirm that the fun-loving spirit enjoyed opening and closing windows and doors and moving objects, just as the salon staff had been experiencing. Once again: coincidence or confirmation? On an even stranger note, long before any paranormal investigation took place at the salon, Justin Barrett had been compelled to name the spirit in his shop Mae. Another coincidence?

Is Justin's of Vero haunted by the original owner of the property? Is she still there, lamenting what was done with the property? Was the spirit of a broken-hearted mother or a mischievous soul who enjoys entertaining the staff responsible for the activity inside the salon? Unfortunately, there is no historical information that could identify who these spirits could have been in life, only the experiences of the living today. Further research and investigation will be needed to uncover the answer.

CHAPTER 7

HALLSTROM HOUSE

Planned before the start of World War I, the Hallstrom home was completed in 1918. Located on the Old Dixie Highway in what is now southern Indian River County, the residence was built by Swedish immigrant Axel Hallstrom. It was to be the culmination of his life's work. The home was built of brick brought down via train from Georgia. Axel's plan was to replicate some of the beautiful homes he had worked at as a gardener in both Chicago and St. Paul.

Born into a farming family in the southern region of Sweden, Axel became a horticulturist and worked, for a period, in the famous Kew Gardens in London. He eventually came to the United States, where he settled in St. Paul, Minnesota. It was there that he met his future wife, Emilia, and they had a daughter, whom they named Ruth. Emilia suffered from tuberculosis, so in 1904, it was decided that the family would move to the new southern frontier of this budding country—Florida. The Hallstrom family traveled by steamboat and train to settle in an area known as the Viking Settlement in current-day northern St. Lucie County, between Fort Pierce and Vero. Today, the area is known as Indrio, where many Scandinavian immigrants settled. Axel planned a palatial home in an area just north of the Viking Settlement known as Oslo. Oslo was another spot where settlers from Norway had begun to build a life. While Axel planned and constructed his new home on Old Dixie Highway, the Hallstrom family lived in a small house directly across the street. Emilia died eight years before the house was completed, leaving Axel as a single parent. Along with this tragedy, World

Aerial view of the Hallstrom House on Old Dixie Highway in southern Indian River County. *Indian River County Historical Society, Bob Bernier.*

War I required the country's supplies and citizens, and thus there was a long delay in the construction. Finally, in 1918, Axel and his young daughter, Ruth, moved into their new home. During this period, Axel's sister, Johanna, came to live with them and help raise Ruth.

Axel went on to become a very successful businessman and grower. While his first crops were pineapple, he later became a citrus grower, bank president and community leader.

Ruth completed high school in Fort Pierce; then, after graduation, her father sent her back to their homeland for finishing school with plans for her to return and attend Florida State College for Women (now known as Florida State University) to fulfill her dream of becoming a teacher. Ruth never made it to college; her Aunt Johanna became ill, and Ruth returned home to become her caretaker as Axel continued to provide for the family. Later, as Axel became elderly, Ruth served as his caretaker until his death in 1966 at the age of ninety-six. Ruth did realize her dream of teaching, for one year, as she became the teacher in a one-room schoolhouse that took an hour to reach by boat in a small village known as Orchid.

Ruth never married. She stayed in the home her father built until she died in 1999 at the age of ninety-five. Ruth had become a fixture in Indian River

County, known for her community involvement and for riding around town in her 1962 Chevrolet Corvette. Ruth's love for her community inspired her to bequeath the stately Victorian-style home in which she grew up to the Indian River Historical Society. She did this so that later generations could see the life of the early pioneers of Indian River County. It is, today, a centerpiece of the society, with regularly scheduled events held there to share a piece of the past.

But have the Hallstroms really left the family home? There are rumors that the home remains occupied by someone—or something—other than the docents of the property or the guests that visit. A former Indian River County deputy sheriff disclosed that he answered a call at the house a number of years ago for an alarm. On his arrival, he heard footsteps and saw movement in the house. Believing there might be a burglary in progress, he entered the building. A search of the home found no evidence of illegal entry and left just the wonderment of a trained law enforcement officer who had clearly experienced an unsettling moment in the home during the middle of the night.

The stories of paranormal activity do not begin or end there. Ruth Stanbridge, Indian River County historian and founder of the Indian River Historical Society, recounts another event. According to Stanbridge, she was present at the Hallstrom House while it was being repaired after Hurricanes Frances and Jeanne devastated the area in 2004. On this day, a crew was working to repair part of the roof. While they were working, Stanbridge left to run an errand.

The workers were up on a ladder that was next to the window of a bedroom on the second floor. They looked in the window and observed an elderly man sitting on the bed in the room. Not wanting to disturb the gentleman, they descended the ladder and were on the ground when Stanbridge returned to the property. When questioned about why they had stopped working, they told Stanbridge that they didn't want to disturb the gentleman who was sitting in his room. Stanbridge informed the workers that there should be no one in the building. They immediately went into the house to check and found no one. The workers confirmed that no one had left the building while they were there. That second-story room happened to be the room that belonged to Axel Hallstrom when he was alive. The workers left and never returned.

Through the generosity of the Indian River County Historical Society and particularly the lead docent of the Hallstrom House, Al Smith, a series of investigations was conducted on the house and property. The results of these investigations provided some interesting clues into the activity others have experienced there over the years.

The presence of children seems to permeate the area, with investigators reporting that they heard children laughing and playing on the grounds. Another investigator reported hearing a disembodied voice while outside saying, "Mommy." It was loud enough for him to identify it as a child's voice. On other occasions, investigators reported seeing figures along the tree line of the property. One occasion, just the legs of a figure were seen in the wooded area on the property's western edge. On two occasions, investigators reported something standing next to them or following closely, accompanied by audible footsteps when no one was there. Shadows have been seen on the front porch where Ruth Hallstrom used to sit in a rocking chair watching carriages and, later, automobiles cruising down the Old Dixie Highway. One investigator reported seeing a man wearing a white shirt and suspenders standing next to the carriage house on the property. Another time, an investigator searching across the road in the old house that the Hallstroms lived in while their brick home was being built had an unsettling experience. He clearly heard a male voice coming from inside what was once the old storage structure. An immediate search for a person inside the structure failed to produce evidence of any living being there.

Is the farmstead built by Axel Hallstrom over a century ago haunted? That is for you to decide. One thing can be said, however, without hesitation: the home and property located at 1723 Old Dixie Highway in Indian River County, Vero Beach, Florida—known as the Hallstrom House—is a place whose history history still lives and thrives.

CHAPTER 8

HERITAGE CENTER / CITRUS MUSEUM

In downtown Vero Beach on Fourteenth Avenue, across from the old courthouse, stands an icon of the early days of Vero Beach, the Heritage Center. Built in 1935, it was a gathering place for the community. During the Second World War, the building was expanded to house a social club for the military personnel stationed at Naval Air Station Vero Beach. Just to the north of the building is a playground known as Pocahontas Park. This park has been a gathering place for Vero Beach's children and families for decades. Prior to it being a children's playground, however, it was a small zoo. This zoo, created in the early 1920s, was home to a variety of different animals. The best-known resident of the zoo was a bear named Alice. Alice was brought to the zoo in 1925, and she eventually passed away there.

After the war, the center continued to be the central gathering spot for events in the city. The room built as a social center for servicemembers was eventually turned into the Indian River County Citrus Museum. During the 1940s, there was a fire inside the main hall of the building that scorched the southeast side of the roof. It was believed to have been started by stage lights that were left on after a dance; the heat from the lights ignited the stage curtains. In the early morning hours, a passerby saw the flames and informed the fire department, saving the building. The burned area was never repaired and can be seen to this day.

The center has been rumored to be haunted for many years. Stories of strange sounds, smells, feelings of being watched and reports of being touched are often discussed among those who have visited the center over

Vero Beach Heritage Center and Citrus Museum. *Larry Lawson.*

the years. This led to a series of investigations by a local paranormal team. In 2016, for example, there was heavy EMF energy detected next to the fireplace on the north side of the hall. There were no electrical outlets or wires or instruments that would have been responsible for the detected energy. About this same time, a large thump was heard toward the back of the stage. An immediate check of the stage area failed to provide any indication of what caused the noise. A search of the outside wall of the building showed that the area where noise came from was over ten feet off the ground. There was no explanation for what had happened.

During another investigation conducted in 2019, several unexplained events occurred inside the building. Investigators observed two shadows moving inside the hall. Several experiments using EMF detectors, flashlights and dowsing rods gave investigators indications that they were not alone. The most significant piece of evidence came during a session to record voices on a digital voice recorder. An investigator asked if anyone had died there. On listening to the recorder, the name Alice was clearly captured. While there was no known person by that name who died there, there was an Alice connected to the property. After hearing this response on the recorder, the director of the Heritage Center, Heather Stapleton, went to her office and retrieved a document identifying who Alice was. Alice, as previously mentioned, was the name of the bear that lived and died at the old zoo next to the center. Was this incident just a coincidence, or was someone reminding us that it wasn't just humans that lived at the site?

Recently, Robyn Berry, the current executive director of the Heritage Center, described not only the feelings of something unseen in the center but also the unmistakable smell of apples and cinnamon in the middle of the open ballroom of the building, when there was nothing there producing the scent.

While the stories of the Heritage Center being haunted have never been conclusively proven, the investigations conducted there and the experiences of guests over the years have not done anything to dispel those rumors. The question remains: Do the spirits of those early days of Vero Beach remain a part of the city's future?

INDIAN RIVER
CHARTER HIGH SCHOOL

Indian River Charter High School was built on the grounds of the old Florida Department of Corrections Probation Officer Academy facility. The land itself is owned by Indian River State College and had been leased to the Florida Department of Corrections. When the academy closed in the 1980s, the property sat vacant until it was leased again, by a group that wanted to develop a charter high school in the area. This consortium of dedicated citizens in Indian River County wanted to build a high school that not only provided the finest traditional high school education but also focused on the visual and performing arts. Thus, Indian River Charter High School was born in 1998.

Throughout the short history of the school, no documented tragic events have occurred there. In the days prior to the Probation Officer Academy and before, it sat as open grounds for cattle and other wildlife.

The original academy building still stands and was renovated for use by Indian River Charter High School for traditional classrooms, physical education, the school library and some administrative functions. It became known by staff and students as the Brick Building.

In 2016, a group of students experienced some unusual activity in their homeroom in the Brick Building. On one occasion when they felt something was amiss, they began to film the room with a cell phone camera and caught a water bottle flying off a shelf by itself. A review of the footage failed to provide any evidence of tampering. The shelf that the bottle came from was up against a wall that did not allow anyone or anything behind the shelf.

Top: Indian River Charter High School. *Larry Lawson.*

Bottom: Indian River Charter High School's brick building prior to its demolition in 2023. *Larry Lawson.*

In the school's black box theater, there is a loft above the space that serves as the class's homeroom area. One of the theater instructors, Alan Darby, was working on the stage one day when he heard loud music coming from the loft area. He asked whoever was up there—nicely, at first—to turn the music down. The music continued to blare loudly. He then made the request again, with more authority, and still did not receive compliance. As Darby went up the stairs to the loft to confront the disobedient student, the music stopped, and he found no one there. There is no way in or out of the loft except for the stairs Darby came up on. This same instructor experienced another incident in the black box theater when, suddenly, small plastic bottles of water were hurled at him from the loft. Again, when Darby went to the loft to find out who was throwing the bottles, he found no one.

In a more recent event, the school's director of information technology, Laura Gaffeny, reported that she was sitting in her office located in the Brick Building when, suddenly, a beverage coaster came flying out of a small slot on the credenza above her desk. This coaster had a rubberized base and was weighted, so it would not have been easily knocked off the shelf. Startled by the coaster landing on her desk, Gaffney commented out loud that there was no need for the office's other "occupants" to "show off." At this comment, another event occurred. Gaffney's nametag, on a lanyard hanging from a peg on her credenza, unexplainably began to sway back and forth. There was no movement or breeze that would have caused this. Laura Gaffney was unable to debunk either event.

On several occasions, the school's security and safety officer clearly heard a voice calling his name and observed shadows in hallways while unlocking the school in the early morning hours. On another occasion, he observed an older-model automobile entering the campus on the west side. On inspection, the vehicle had disappeared. The only way it could have left was via the same drive it came in.

During an investigation conducted by a local paranormal team that was invited to see if there was any truth to the stories, some interesting events occurred. While no tangible evidence was collected, one investigator claimed to have been touched, and shadows were reported in several areas on the campus. The most intriguing experience was had by a school official who was present during the investigation. The assistant school director, present for the investigation, was with one team investigating the Brick Building. While at this location, he began to hear talking coming from inside the library, next to the same area where the bottle was videotaped flying from a shelf. Checking the library area, he found no one and could find no logical explanation for the voices he heard.

In a more recent encounter, the school's facility director, Shawn MacDonald, described an event that has left him baffled to this day. He observed what appeared to be an older gentleman walking next to the Brick Building. Because it was five thirty in the morning, he was concerned about someone else being on campus. As he approached the area where he saw this person, he found that no one was there. Concerned that someone who appeared elderly had possibly fallen and injured themselves, he combed the location looking for this individual. After again not finding anyone, MacDonald checked the security cameras in that area of the campus. The cameras provided a complete recorded view of the area in question during the time he saw the man walking through. What the cameras did not capture was the man that MacDonald clearly saw walking next to the building. So who did he see? Perhaps it was the residual energy of a person who had walked the area in the past or, maybe, a returning spirit checking on the state of the property he once owned.

So is this institution of learning haunted by students of the past, or are the former inhabitants of the area returning to see what has been done with their home? Only further inquiry will tell.

CHAPTER 10

TANGELO HOUSE APARTMENTS

The Ryburn Apartment Building on Royal Palm Boulevard in Vero Beach was originally built in the mid-1920s by Thomas Ryburn; construction was completed in 1926. It was one of four similarly built apartment buildings in the Royal Palm Subdivision. One of these identical apartments was constructed directly across the street. The building remained an apartment complex throughout its history, becoming known as the Tangelo Apartments in the 1950s. The last official occupants vacated the apartments in approximately 2010, and the building was abandoned and fell into ruin. In 2021, it was purchased by Garrett and Stephanie Puzzo. The Puzzos purchased the property with the intention of returning it to its original purpose as an apartment building while retaining its historical significance.

As work began on the property, Garrett Puzzo and his construction crew began to feel an unexplained energy in the building. The construction crew began to notice tools being moved or going missing altogether. The incidents became common enough that the construction crew placed a cross on the wall of one of the apartments to appease any uneasy spirits still inhabiting the building. With the continuing unexplained incidents at the apartment, Garrett Puzzo invited a local paranormal team to come in and investigate the property. Over a period that spanned almost two years, the paranormal investigative team is said to have experienced numerous events that gave them little doubt there was something out of the ordinary happening at the Tangelo Apartments. During these investigations, shadows and voices

Tangelo Apartments in Vero Beach. Known as the Ryburn Apartments when built in 1924, it was well known for unexplained activity during its remodeling. *Larry Lawson.*

were recorded. On several occasions, both investigators and guests of the owners have felt ill or dizzy, been touched and, in one incident, passed out. Figures were regularly captured on the team's SLS camera system. In one incident with the SLS camera, a figure was seen on the second floor, and it was observed, on camera, suddenly kneeling down as if trying to hide.

During the later stages of the reconstruction, one member of the team working for Garrett Puzzo, Brandon Hunt, was staying in the apartments. Brandon tells an interesting story that he relayed to this author. As he slept in a room next to the front interior stairs, Brandon noticed that the light on the staircase kept coming on and going off. The light was set to detect motion on the stairway and was brand new, just installed. When Brandon came out and looked, he found nothing—no creatures of any kind. Thinking it might possibly have been a small animal that had scampered off, he went back to bed, leaving the door to the hall and stairwell open. Not long afterward, he saw a shadow, the height of a small person, walk past the door. This time, he loudly announced to whoever or whatever was there, "Stop it!" He had no other issues that night.

A grand opening event was held after construction was completed on the apartments. Many officials from the City of Vero Beach and the Indian

River Historical Society were in attendance to welcome the building back to life. The community turnout for the event was enormous, as many came to take an historical tour of the property. But during the event, it appeared that past residents also wanted to be recognized. Guests reported strange feelings of being watched and even being touched. Another attendee who had rented an apartment there decades ago reported that the building was haunted even back when she lived there.

Do the past residents of one of the oldest apartment buildings in Vero Beach still believe that this is their home? Or are they just waiting to greet the new tenants as they move in?

CHAPTER 11
BARBECUE CHARLIE

It was April 6, 1950, and residents and visitors to Vero Beach and Indian River County saw it as just another idyllic day in the place "where the tropics begin." But on one of the many islands that dot the intercoastal waterway known as the Indian River, something evil was destined to happen.

The Barber Bridge sits at the southern end of the city of Vero Beach, connecting the mainland to the barrier island. Several hundred yards north of the bridge sat an island, one of the many places known as "spoil islands." On this particular island lived two older fishermen named Charles Chapman and Charles Shrewsbury. Shrewsbury, age fifty-seven, had moved to the island to enjoy a life of solitude and fishing. Despite this, he still had friends he spent time with. Chapman, on the other hand, was almost twenty years older than Shrewsbury and well known to the Vero Beach Police Department for his public drunkenness.

Friends of Shrewsbury had been looking for him and were concerned when he could not be found. These friends had contacted the police department to report him missing. Officers were sent out to the island to investigate and were met by Chapman. When asked by the officers if he knew where Charlie Shrewsbury was, Chapman told them that Shrewsbury had gone to Miami to buy some new clothes and would return in about two weeks. The officers took him at his word and left. After some time had passed with still no sign of Charlie Shrewsbury, his friends returned to the police department, demanding that they search for him. It is said that the chief of police, along with his chief of detectives, went back out to the island to seek more information from Chapman. Not finding Chapman or Shrewsbury on the island, they began to search. What they found was typical of a fisherman's lair: shacks, fishing boats, nets, large metal oil drums, fishing poles and supplies. They did note that Shrewsbury's boat was still there. While searching through Chapman's area, the chief noted a box near an old shack. When he picked it up, he found ashes and a gold-capped tooth. The officers had a bad feeling. After returning to the police station, the chief of police contacted the Indian River County Sheriff's Office because the island sat outside the jurisdiction of the City of Vero Beach. Investigation into the contents of the box continued. Veterans' records from the U.S. government revealed that Charlie Shrewsbury actually did have a tooth with a gold crown similar to the one found in the box. Orders went out to find Charlie Chapman and bring him in.

Old Charlie Chapman was found drunk in a local saloon and brought in. When they were ready, the officers and sheriff's deputies on the case questioned Chapman about the tooth and what he knew about Shrewsbury's disappearance. It didn't take Chapman long to confess that, yes, he did know what happened the night Charlie Shrewsbury disappeared.

Chapman explained that he and Shrewsbury were drinking and got into an argument over their boats striking each other and causing some slight damage. Chapman claimed that Shrewsbury picked up a tool known as a grubbing axe and came at him. Chapman picked up a piece of wood and threw it at Shrewsbury with enough force to knock him to the ground. When Chapman approached Shrewsbury, lying on the ground, and checked him, he saw that Shrewsbury was dead. Chapman began to panic. After a short while, he decided that instead of calling the police, he would chop up the remains of Charlie Shrewsbury, put his dismembered body parts in the old oil drum near his shack and cook them in it. Charlie Chapman was arrested and eventually convicted of manslaughter. He was sent to state prison for fifteen years, serving eight of them before being released. He returned to his shack and quietly died there in 1969 at the age of ninety-five. He is buried in a crudely marked grave in the Winter Beach Cemetery just south of Sebastian.

While Charlie Chapman's story did explain the death, and his admission confirmed why Shrewsbury's remains were found at his fishing shack in the condition they were in, there were still questions. Chapman was over seventy years of age at the time of the incident. How was a man his age able to pick up a big enough log and throw it with enough energy to kill Charlie Shrewsbury? How was it that Shrewsbury was unable to duck out of the way? And how was it that when the log hit him, it killed him instantly? What about the rumors that Shrewsbury had come into some money, which Chapman found out about and killed Shrewsbury for? And why did Chapman treat Shrewsbury's body the way he did, especially if he killed him in self-defense? There were only two people present when the death occurred. One was burned to ashes and left unceremoniously in a box. The other claimed it was self-defense. What really happened that night on the quiet stretches of the Indian River? Oddly, local citizens who saw the fire on the beach of Cremation Point reported to police that they believed a witches' coven was conducting a magical ceremony there. The truth will never be known.

While there are no documented cases of paranormal activity at Cremation Point, this just another example of how the evil and unfathomable can occur even in the most serene of locations.

PART II
SEBASTIAN AND ROSELAND: A HISTORY

In 1605, Captain Álvaro Mexía, a Spanish military officer, cartographer and well-known explorer, was sent by the Spanish governor of Florida in St. Augustine to meet with the Ais. Captain Mexía's orders were to build a trade agreement with them. It was this meeting that led to the Spanish naming the area for Saint Sebastian and the first recorded encounter with the Ais people. Sebastian saw permanent settlers in the 1850s, but it was not until the 1880s that the area experienced any substantial growth and development. The Saint Sebastian area became well known as a fishing village.

An English immigrant and retired minister named Thomas New called the area Newhaven in 1882 and opened the first post office in the area. New became the first postmaster that same year. Just two years later, in 1884, Thomas New ran afoul of government officials who claimed he abused his authority as postmaster. As a result of these accusations, he was removed from his position and a new postmaster, August Park, was temporarily appointed. The Reverend New stayed in the area after his dismissal and later became ill. He died in Sebastian in 1885. Reverend New's influence on the history of Sebastian is discussed later in this chapter in more detail.

Another newcomer to the area was Sylvanus Kitching, who arrived in 1883. Kitching was eventually named the permanent postmaster, replacing August Park. Kitching was the person responsible for renaming the area Sebastian, in honor of its original Spanish name. It was after 1885 that Sebastian's development had begun, under the influence of other families, whose names would become synonymous with the area—Groves, Kroegel, Park, Hardee, Sembler, Rose, Lawson (no relation to this author) and Vickers, just to name a few. Sebastian became a center of activity in this new land. Sebastian's reputation as a thriving fishing village continued to bring new settlers to the area.

Roseland, a neighboring community, was developing simultaneously with Sebastian, having a post office and becoming recognized as a town in 1892. The entire area was known for its fishing and its agricultural products, including citrus, vegetables, sugarcane and pineapples.

In 1893, Henry Flagler's railroad came to town and helped the expansion. It was then that A.O. Russell built a narrow-gauge railroad track from Flagler's line through Sebastian to a plot of land he was developing called Cincinnatus. Cincinnatus was later to become known as Fellsmere, Florida. Russell was a well-known figure in the printing industry. He was also one of the founders of a company that became known worldwide as Bicycle Playing Cards. Sebastian was becoming the hub of activity and change in the area.

In 1905, the area just south of the Sebastian Inlet was given to the newly created St. Lucie County. Sebastian and Roseland became the northernmost border of St. Lucie County. The future of Sebastian was being laid out. The first street in Sebastian was Louisiana Avenue, which ran parallel to Flagler's railroad tracks. Main Street was to follow, and construction of the town's first school was completed in 1887 on Louisiana Avenue, near the new train depot.

In 1924, Sebastian was officially incorporated as a city. In 1925, Indian County was created out of the northern area of St. Lucie County, and finally, the citizens of Sebastian could chart their own destiny. To this day, Roseland is still unincorporated but remains a vibrant community.

The history of Sebastian and Roseland runs deep and can still be enjoyed by residents and visitors alike. Without question, some of those who brought life to the northern end of Indian River County still want their voices heard.

CHAPTER 1

BEYOND USELESS BOUTIQUE

In 1913, before Sebastian was incorporated into a municipality, its original town hall was built by an organization known as the Woodmen of the World. This building, located on present-day US Highway 1 just a few blocks south of Main Street, became the center of this growing little fishing village that was later to become the city of Sebastian. It was not only the town hall but also a theater, a concert hall, a home and, at one point, a Masonic temple. Through years of storms, municipal development and cultural changes, this building has withstood the test of time. Today, it is an eclectic store owned by Richard Robinson and his late wife, Lisanne, known as the Beyond Useless Boutique.

Lisanne and Richard had shared with Sebastian police officer Ashley Penn that the building was rife with paranormal activity. They described feeling others present when there was no one else in the building. They also saw unexplained shadows and noises they could not identify. Patrons who entered the shop often spoke to Lisanne and Richard about feeling that there was something else, some other entity, in the store. Richard and Lisanne went on to note that similar activities had been experienced in the home next to the Beyond Useless Boutique that was built by early Sebastian residents Parris and Balmar Lawson. It was brought to the attention of local paranormal investigators, who expressed an interest in investigating the claims further.

The history of the building leads one to believe that energy left behind by those in the past may very well still be with us today. When Lisanne

The Beyond Useless Boutique in Sebastian, Florida. Built in 1913 by the Woodmen of the World organization, it was Sebastian's first town hall. *Larry Lawson.*

first purchased the building and began to renovate it, she made a discovery that indicated perhaps earlier occupants of the building may have sensed a ghostly presence. While working in the bathroom on the first floor, Lisanne found a magazine left hidden in the wooden rafters of the ceiling. The magazine was dated October 1927 and was titled *Ghost Stories*.

Why was this magazine from almost one hundred years ago found inside the ceiling? Was it because others experienced paranormal activity in the building back then? Did those who inhabited the building in those early years conduct activities that allowed beings from other dimensions to travel between our world and theirs? Or were they simply interested in the same topic that has mystified us since the dawn of humankind—ghosts?

During one of the paranormal examinations of the building, investigators experienced some of the same types of phenomena that the Robinsons had reported. Their equipment kept the investigators guessing about who they were communicating with, but it was the eerie feeling of being watched that caught their attention. One team member was using dowsing rods in the attic of the building and received some very distinct answers from an entity that claimed to be a teenage girl. An SLS camera positioned in front of a team member showed a figure next to him. But the answers to the team's questions came on the dowsing rods. The figure seen on the SLS camera began responding to the questions, and its answers paralleled those received on the dowsing rods. One of the investigators also reported that he was touched, and others on the team claimed to have seen the shadow of a short-statured person in the workroom on the bottom floor of the building. Later investigations of the building produced similar phenomena.

Lisanne, a guiding force in the artistic community of Sebastian, passed away in 2019. Richard continues as an important member of the community, caring for one of the most iconic buildings in Sebastian.

Do the citizens of an earlier time in Sebastian still visit their town hall and community center? Next time you visit Sebastian, come by and visit this historic building. You may encounter something you can't explain. But that is nothing compared to the house that sits next door to it.

CHAPTER 2
PARRIS AND BAMMA LAWSON HOME

In 1888, twelve-year-old Parris Lawson left the family home in Quitman, Georgia, with two others to bring his family's belongings to the site of their new home in what is now Sebastian. In 1889, the rest of the family arrived, becoming some of the earliest homesteaders in the area. They were followed a few years later in 1907 by another family from the same area of Georgia, the Vickerses. In fact, the families were well acquainted. Parris and one of the Vickers daughters, Balmar, who was called "Bamma," would later marry.

The marriage between Paris Lawson and Bamma Vickers came in July 1908. Parris built a home for Bamma east of the railroad tracks, facing west, near the original downtown area of Sebastian. In 1911, the home was finished and the Lawsons moved in. It was in this home that Parris and Bamma would become two of the most influential members of Sebastian society.

In 1919, Bamma's parents, Stephen and Sarah Vickers, built a home on a northern lot next door to Parris and Bamma's residence, facing the east along the road that would later become part of US Highway 1. That same year, Parris moved his and Bamma's house away from the tracks approximately 150 yards, turned it to face east and sat it next to that of Bamma's parents. Both houses remain in the same place today. While the old Vickers home is the residence of another family, the Bamma Lawson house is owned by Richard Robinson of the Beyond Useless Boutique.

The Lawson home became the center of much activity in Sebastian over the years, as both Parris and Bamma became leaders within the community.

The home of Parris and Balmar (Bamma) Lawson, Sebastian, Florida. *Larry Lawson.*

Parris was to become the city clerk for Sebastian, the city election supervisor and a city councilman. Bamma was active in many civic organizations and was a founding member of the Sebastian Women's Club in 1914. Many feel that the most significant contribution made to the area by Parris and Bamma was the creation of the first children's library in the county, built and maintained in their home.

The house still sits on the same property that it has been on since it was moved in 1919. The house as it is now has been used by the Robinsons as a vacation rental over the years for visitors wanting to enjoy the laid-back life of Sebastian. It has also been used by family members who were visiting. And these guests have also had the pleasure of getting to know the first occupants of the home.

As Richard Robinson recounts, the experiences of past guests in the Bamma Lawson house include hearing footsteps on the stairs at night, seeing shadows moving within the building and observing objects being moved. The most significant event to have taken place in the house was a footstool being moved during the night and the apparition of a woman, believed to be Bamma Lawson, sitting on a small couch in the family room on the first floor. According to Richard, many who have stayed there have reported similar events. Richard stated that even his brother experienced the same type of phenomena while visiting. One night during a stay, he came down the stairs to use the restroom. As he was returning to his room, he found that a small couch that was in the room had been moved by someone, or something, so that it was now blocking the stairway back to the bedrooms.

Because of the property's location near the railroad tracks, Richard was approached by an amateur treasure hunter who wanted to search behind both the Lawson home and the Beyond Useless Boutique. He was hoping to find historical artifacts there, because much of the business and pedestrian activity in early Sebastian occurred along these tracks. Richard allowed him to search the backyard of the Lawson house. This area included where the house originally stood before it was moved the 150 yards east in 1919. Richard was unsure if anything was hidden in the ground but allowed the gentleman to try.

During his search, the treasure hunter was able to locate a small metal emblem with the initials "W.O.W." on it buried in the earth. Research later revealed that the plaque was from the early nineteenth century. These emblems were used as markers that were placed on the gravestones of deceased members of the fraternal organization Woodmen of the World. This was the same group that constructed the original town hall that is now the Beyond Useless Boutique, which sits next door and is also owned by Richard Robinson. This emblem is so unique in its purpose that finding it there led the treasure hunter to believe a grave might actually exist on the property.

That was not the only unusual thing that occurred during his endeavor. The treasure hunter also reported that all his electronic equipment began to inexplicably malfunction. Battery-powered metal detectors that had just received new batteries or fully charged ones were showing that their power was drained. When he walked off the property to his car, the gear started functioning again. He also was able to find indications of metal in the ground that would then move on him. He reported these events to Richard, who advised him to contact a paranormal investigation team. Even after describing what he experienced with his equipment to the investigators, no logical explanation for what happened to him could be found.

During an investigation into the residence, investigators were able to document several interesting experiences. A spirit box captured several voices that were not considered to be radio interference. A male voice was heard to say, "Thank you for coming," followed shortly afterward by a female voice saying, "Go away." In the upstairs bedroom that had a bathroom attached, EMF meters recorded numerous unexplained spikes. When opening a closet door in the same bedroom, a team member experienced a sudden and significant temperature drop that could not be explained. The SLS camera used by the team caught a figure that was next to another investigator. When it was asked to touch him, an audio recording of the event revealed a female voice saying, "Oh, sure."

Follow-up investigations, as well as guests' experiences, continued to provide these same types of incidents, whether they were asked for or not.

Could there be a hundred-year-old grave belonging to a deceased member of Woodmen of the World behind the Bamma Lawson house? Are Parris and Bamma Lawson coming back to check on their property—or perhaps they never left? Either way, the activity that continues in the home of one Sebastian's pioneer families cannot be denied or explained.

CHAPTER 3

SEBASTIAN WOMEN'S CLUB

The Sebastian Women's Club was formed in 1914. The club's first president was Sarah Wentworth Rose, wife of the town's physician, Dr. David Rose. Sarah came to Sebastian in 1908 with her new husband and within a short time became an outspoken leader in the community, particularly in the area of literacy. Her desire to improve the life of this community led Sarah to the create the Sebastian Women's Club in her home in 1914. The meetings were held in the town hall (currently the Beyond Useless Boutique).

Sarah Rose continued to lead the women's club during those early days until her untimely death from a car accident in 1927. A short time after she was elected president of the County Federation of Women's Clubs, she was traveling with her husband, Dr. David Rose, on Dixie Highway when their automobile collided with another, killing Sarah. While the occupants of the other vehicle were taken to the closest hospital in Fort Pierce, Dr. Rose elected to take Sarah to their home, where they were both treated for their injuries by colleagues of Dr. Rose. Unfortunately, Sarah succumbed to her injuries.

The club had been engaging in fundraising to build a clubhouse of its own, but the beginnings of the impending Great Depression (1929–33) were felt, and the club's money was lost in the closing of the banks that held it. With the loss of their beloved president, Sarah, the rest of the club's membership was determined to raise the money and find volunteer labor to complete the project. In 1928, the permanent home of the Sebastian Women's Club was completed by local volunteers. In honor of Sarah Wentworth Rose, the new

Sebastian River Junior Women's Club. *Larry Lawson.*

clubhouse came to fruition, and it remains standing in the same spot today. Later in 1928, Dr. Rose married Elizabeth Wegener, a longtime friend of his deceased wife. Elizabeth was also elected, for a term, president of the club.

The club has remained an active civic association to this day. Its work in youth literacy and assisting families in need continues the legacy of Sarah Wentworth Rose and all those who built the Sebastian Women's Club.

Some say that these early members of the club may still be attending meetings. One of these members, former club president Teddy Hulse, claims that the clubhouse has been the location of some unusual activity over the years. According to Hulse, a mist has been seen in the corner of the meeting room several times, there were unexplained noises and the feeling that they were not alone has been constant over the years.

In September 2019, the Sebastian Women's Club opened its doors to investigators to check the building and determine if some of their deceased members were indeed still present.

This investigation brought to light some interesting issues and created even more questions. After examining the activity in the building, the investigators were left with the clear belief that at least two spirits inhabited it: Sarah and Elizabeth, not only connected in life but also in the afterlife, as they were both married to Dr. David Rose.

Sebastian River Junior Women's Club meeting room. *Larry Lawson.*

During the investigation, information from the team's investigative equipment made it evident that neither of Dr. Rose's past wives wanted to leave the building that they cared so dearly about. What was once a friendship appeared to disintegrate into animosity in the afterlife. One clear example of this was during sessions where dowsing rods and EMF detectors were being used simultaneously. During these sessions, the dowsing rods and the EMF detectors were answering at the same time and corroborating each other, suggesting that these two old friends were now angry with each other, perhaps over their shared affection for Dr. Rose. Sarah was asked if she was upset that Dr. Rose married Elizabeth after her death. The dowsing rods gave a resounding yes. Likewise, investigators asked Elizbeth if she was unhappy with Sarah remaining in the building. Again, the equipment gave a clear answer: yes. This type of evidence gave the investigators confidence that they were getting answers. On another occasion, investigators asked the entity that was there to point the rods toward where they were standing. Both rods moved in unison to the same spot. The investigator holding the rods changed position, and the question was again asked about where the spirit stood. The rods again pointed to the same spot in the room where the entity stated it was.

Is the love and passion for their community so strong that past members of the Sebastian Women's Club are still looking out for its future endeavors? Or is the lingering energy just the animosity between two women who loved the same man?

CHAPTER 4

PAREIDOLIA BREWERY

The land on Cleveland Street, off US Highway 1 in Sebastian, sat vacant for years until 1964, when the U.S. Postal Service constructed the new Sebastian Post Office. Once built, it served the Sebastian community until it closed in 1991, when the new post office was built on Main Street. The building sat empty until 1997, when it was purchased and the first of two hardware stores occupied the site. In 2017, the building was sold to the current owner, who then leased it to the owners of Pareidolia Brewery. Pareidolia is a local craft brewery owned by Peter "Pete" and Lynn Anderson. The brewery was originally established in another part of Sebastian, but when the old post office became available, the Andersons saw this as a perfect opportunity to move to a better location.

Once Pete and his team began to convert the old post office into the brewery, they noticed strange things happening. Activity such as shadows and unexplained noises became common in the new brewery, but it was one event that began to make Pete wonder exactly what was happening.

One day, Pete and the property's owner, Tom Haynes, were working inside the building to prepare it for opening. Suddenly, they both heard a loud crashing sound. Pete said that the crash was so loud he first thought that a vehicle had crashed into the building. He also worried about a possible explosion in the brewery area. An examination of the facility showed nothing unusual. Nothing had crashed into the building, exploded or even fallen. The cause of the noise was never found, yet it was heard clearly by both men.

Originally built in 1960 as a U.S. post office, this is now the home of Pareidolia Brewery in Sebastian, Florida. *Larry Lawson*.

The bar at Pareidolia Brewery. *Larry Lawson*.

Once the brewery opened, more activity was noticed. There were sounds of dishes crashing in the food preparation area and doors opening in the restrooms when no one was in there. Shadows and possible apparitions have also been seen in the building. Pete has witnessed both a sign unexplainedly flying off a shelf and a clipboard coming off a wall in the brew room. The activity was becoming so common that Pete and his staff gave the name Frank to whatever unknown entity was causing it. Pete went so far as to name one of his craft beers after the entity, calling it Frank's Farmhouse. One interesting note is that all the activity experienced by Pete and others has been during the daytime hours.

At the invitation of Pete Anderson, a local paranormal team conducted a daytime investigation of the Pareidolia Brewery. While videotaping a session in the main dining area, the team experienced the first of several unexplained phenomena. An investigator was standing near the front entrance of the brewery, about one to two feet away from the wall. He suddenly heard several distinct musical notes. He asked if anyone else in the room had heard them, and they had not. An immediate review of the videotape and an audio recorder revealed that there were approximately six notes that sounded like a piano. On the wall directly behind the investigator, there was a ukulele hanging on display. The ukulele strings were strummed, and the sound was not the same as the notes that had been recorded. There was little question that the musical notes were those of a piano. There is no piano in the building and no known record of a piano ever being located there. Could the musical notes have come from the ukulele that was hanging on that wall? Possibly. If so, someone still would have had to strum the strings of the instrument. How could that have happened? Attempts to recreate the event failed to reproduce what had occurred. It could not be debunked.

During the rest of the investigation, active listening sessions with the spirit box produced the names Frank (the name given to the entity by Pete Anderson) and Larry. But it was the EVP sessions that produced the final bit of evidence in the investigation. When the team reviewed the recorded sessions, they heard unidentified voices that were caught on the recording devices. One voice was heard to say, "You're talking too much." Another was heard saying the name David. More musical notes were also recorded. But the one EVP recording that caught the team's interest the most was of two words, spoken by a voice that didn't belong to any investigator in the room. The words were: "I'll murder."

A visit to the Pareidolia Brewery in Sebastian is a wonderful way to enjoy the hospitality of the Treasure Coast. Guests come from all around Indian River County and beyond to take in the pleasant, friendly atmosphere found at the Pareidolia Brewery. And who knows, Frank himself might just join you to provide some additional entertainment.

CHAPTER 5
MEL FISHER'S TREASURE MUSEUM

In 1927, the Letchworth Garage was built and put to use by Rabun Letchworth. Years later, it became the home of the Sebastian Fire Department and Volunteer Ambulance Squad. In 1992, a treasure museum was opened in the building honoring the work of world-famous treasure hunter Mel Fisher. While Fisher became famous for his discovery of the Spanish treasure ship *Atocha* off the Florida Keys in 1969, his early work included salvaging treasure off the coast of Sebastian from the Spanish treasure fleet that sank in a hurricane in July 1715. This very disaster, and the treasures it left behind, led to this area's nickname, the Treasure Coast. The Mel Fisher Treasure Museum was opened by Fisher's daughter, Taffi Fisher Abt, and the museum remains one of the Sebastian's most popular attractions. Today, the museum is managed by Taffi's daughter, Nichole Johanson.

Stories of strange happenings inside the museum circulate locally. The apparition of a child had been reported as being seen in the gift shop area of the museum by staff. There is another report of a bust of Mel Fisher turning on its own.

Because of the activity experienced there by staff, the local paranormal team was asked to come and investigate the strange occurrences. Perhaps some of the most compelling evidence from the initial investigation was collected during a dowsing rod session in the theater of the museum. While an investigator was conducting the session, it was believed that contact was made with Mel Fisher himself. While the investigators were asking Fisher

Mel Fisher's Treasure Museum. *Larry Lawson.*

questions, museum manager and Mel Fisher's granddaughter Nichole Johanson entered the room. The investigator paused and asked Fisher if he could identify anyone in the room who was related to him by pointing the rods at the person. The dowsing rods immediately turned toward a stunned Johanson and pointed directly at her. This investigation also provided many incidents in which team members witnessed numerous light anomalies and shadows throughout the entire building.

During several investigations of the museum, the paranormal research team has been able to experience numerous unexplainable events that confirmed some of the claims made by museum staff: moving figures were seen on the security cameras, shadows or flashes of something moving in the rooms, cold breezes that were not related to the air-conditioning system and mists appearing in the theater. One interesting EVP even led to a possible contact with a former firefighter. When the investigators asked if there was anyone with them, a voice was heard on the spirit box saying, "I'm a firefighter." Perhaps this entity was from the era when the building served as the headquarters for the town's volunteer fire department.

In another incident, a senior investigator said she clearly saw the shadow of a small figure, the size of a child, run by a glass display case. Another piece of evidence collected during this investigation was a figure caught on the SLS camera standing next to another investigator. On the investigator's request, the figure captured on camera turned and reached out to him.

It seems that the Mel Fisher Treasure Museum in Sebastian is not only home to many of the treasures and artifacts of Mel Fisher's life and adventures but may also be the home of spirits attached to those artifacts and those who have occupied the building in bygone years.

CHAPTER 6
LAPORTE FARMS

L aPorte Farms, located in the unincorporated Roseland area next to Sebastian, has been known for many years as a family-oriented farm and petting zoo where visitors come to enjoy animals and nature. Opened in 1994 by Laura LaPorte, it has become well known as a destination for public events and school field trips.

LaPorte Farms' history is somewhat darker than today's view of this happy place. The property has what is believed by many to be the oldest, and smallest, cemetery in the county. It has also been said that a severe fire once burned through the property, uncovering the hidden graveyard and also possibly killing several children in a home on the property at the same time. Some believe that the graves on the property were the final resting spots for the local postmaster's mail-order brides.

Historical research has failed to substantiate many of these claims. While a small cemetery containing six graves was found on the property, no information exists to suggest that they belonged to the mail-order brides of local legend. Research did show that there was a fire on the property in 1971 that revealed the remains of six people buried there. Legend also suggests that in the 1930s, there was a house on the property that burned and six children died in the blaze. Historical research revealed no record of a home burning or the deaths of any children as the result of a fire. The cemetery today has been consolidated by Laura LaPorte in an area of the farm with the respect and reverence due to a place of final rest.

Despite the historical record debunking some of the legends about the property, there have been reports of paranormal activity that just cannot be ignored. Of these reports, the most common were of keys being moved and apparitions seen in the main house, adding to the paranormal intrigue found on LaPorte Farms. One of the workers, who would occasionally spend the night on the farm, reported hearing booted footsteps on the front porch of the main house, followed by his name being called out when no one was there. There is also the report from the son of a former employee who told his father that one evening, he saw someone walk up to the window of the main house and then walk away. A check of the area revealed that there was no one there.

On another occasion, a boy aged about nine reported an older "bald man" who walked by and peered into the doorway, only to turn away.

Given these stories and legends, a team of researchers was given the opportunity to investigate these claims during the winter of 2019. The team would not be disappointed.

During the investigation, electromagnetic field (EMF) activity was detected in areas where no electric interference should have been. This included an EVP session where an EMF detector lit up whenever the subject of the cemetery was brought up.

But it was the barn area on the property that proved to be the most active during the investigation. While working inside, a senior investigator on the team asked if someone was behind her while she was conducting an experiment with the spirit box. Her eyes and ears were covered so that she could not see or hear anything other than words from the device. There was no one behind her, and she later explained it felt as though a "large presence" was behind her.

The interior of the barn was under static camera coverage during the investigation. While the team was in the barn, investigators at the command post monitoring the camera's activity observed a rod of light as it floated to most of the other investigators in area. At first, it was believed to be a cobweb or similar debris that was floating back and forth, but the movement looked deliberate. Further examination of the area revealed no cobwebs or spiderwebs were responsible for the phenomenon. The light was also observed by another team member who ensured the event was recorded. The cameras recorded the light as it went from investigator to investigator, stopping and disappearing into one of them—not to be seen again. When the team examined the footage, they saw the rod of light at one point going into the middle of the barn and stopping in front of a horse stall. A horse appeared out of the stall, looked at the light and retreated into the stall. At the same time, the light moved away from the horse and back to the table where the investigators were sitting. Despite close examination by several investigators, no logical explanation was found.

It was also in the barn that a figure was captured on the SLS camera. This figure appeared to be lying on the table with its legs crossed. While the team observed the figure, they asked it to reach up and hold the hand of one of the investigators, which it did several times. The team was unable to debunk this event, either.

The unusual history of LaPorte Farms and the reports of paranormal activity are both intriguing and chilling. To this day, there are more questions than answers about the history and haunting of LaPorte Farms.

CHAPTER 7
CRAB-E-BILL'S / HURRICANE HARBOR RESTAURANT / McCAIN'S GARAGE

In 1925, the Prohibition era, in which alcohol was illegal in the United States, was in full swing. During this time, citizens were highly restricted in both possessing and selling alcohol. But off the Florida coast lay islands that were governed by other countries. The islands of the Bahamas, for instance, were under the British flag. It is only about one hundred miles between Freeport, Bahamas, and Sebastian. Americans looking to enjoy a drink, and those wanting to make a profit from that desire, turned to these Caribbean islands to satisfy their needs. Alcohol smuggling became as common as the brewing of moonshine in the stills found in the swamps and glades of Florida. And it was a lucrative business.

Also in 1925, Jess Powell built an auto repair garage on property that is today found on the 1500 block of N. Indian River Drive in Sebastian. Two years later, in 1927, this garage was purchased from him by Robert "Bob" McCain, a known bootlegger and smuggler. McCain expanded the garage all the way back to the waterline on the Indian River. He also added a dock extending into the river. But this was no ordinary dock. This dock was built so that smaller boats could maneuver underneath it. It was also equipped with a trapdoor. This allowed boats to deliver illegal alcohol from the islands to a new and innovative hiding place. The dock and trapdoor were built in such a way that the deliveries could not be seen from the street. McCain would then use a hidden room in the back of the garage to keep his merchandise away from the eyes of law enforcement officials.

The former car garage used by bootlegger Robert McCain during Prohibition. It later became the Hurricane Harbor and then the Crab-E-Bill's Restaurant. *Larry Lawson.*

Across the street from the garage, Bob McCain built the home that his family lived in. But this house was not built only as a sanctuary for his wife and their children. Hidden underneath the house, accessible only through a hidden trapdoor, was a small cellar McCain used to hide his illegal goods. With this, he was able to elude arrest for years.

In 1930, McCain was finally caught and arrested by federal agents. Arrested with him was the sheriff of Indian River County, Joel Knight. He was convicted and sent to prison in Georgia, sentenced to thirteen months. He was later released and died in St. Augustine, Florida, in 1953.

This was not the end of the McCain saga, however. McCain's youngest son, David Lucius McCain, became the pride of the family. He graduated from law school at the University of Florida in 1955 and later served as an officer in the United States Air Force. He was later appointed to the Florida Supreme Court, where he was the youngest justice ever to serve. During his time as a Florida Supreme Court justice, however, he was accused of unethical activity ranging from receiving improper campaign contributions to providing favored rulings for friends and acquaintances. He was also accused of excessive drinking and bribery. Due to these allegations, he resigned from the supreme court in 1975 and was disbarred in 1978. Like his father, he later became a smuggler. Unlike his father, however, alcohol was not his choice of illegal contraband—instead, he chose narcotics. David McCain was indicted on four felony counts of narcotics smuggling. He skipped bail in 1983 and failed to show up in court as ordered. He lived the rest of his life on the run from the law. Research reveals that he died of cancer in Jacksonville, Florida, under an assumed name, in 1986.

The home built by McCain remained across from the garage until 1990, when it was demolished. In the 1960s, after lying abandoned for years, the garage became a seafood and oyster packing plant. In 1978, the property was renovated and became the Hurricane Harbor Restaurant, a well-known Sebastian eatery. The restaurant later, under new management, was renamed "Crab-E-Bill's." In 2008, the City of Sebastian took ownership of the property for waterfront development, but Crab-E-Bill's Restaurant remains.

Before the home was torn down in 1990, stories of it being haunted circulated around the area. Occupants and visitors to the house recounted hearing footsteps on the stairs and seeing shadows near the area of the trapdoor used to gain entrance to McCain's secret cellar. The residents also claimed they had the uneasy feeling of being watched. An investigation by a team of journalists in 1988 failed to confirm many of these reports. The journalists did find that the atmosphere in the residence was uncomfortable.

The garage-turned-restaurant is also rumored to be the permanent home of smugglers and bootleggers. Reports over the years say that shadowy figures are still seen on the dock where the illegal alcohol was unloaded, and employees of the restaurants have also reported shadows and uneasy feelings of being watched.

The McCain home and business defined, fairly or not, the family's legacy. One has to wonder if all the activity that is still witnessed is the result of that legacy or the energy left behind by everything that occurred there.

CHAPTER 8
SIMEON PARK HOME

Simeon Park was born in 1877 to Sebastian pioneers August and Polly Ann Park. It is claimed that Simeon was the first White child born in this part of Florida. His father, August Park, was a fisherman who had emigrated from Germany. His mother was from North Carolina. August Park was one of the original landowners in Sebastian, and part of the property he owned was later donated to Sebastian as the city's cemetery off North US Highway 1.

Simeon Park became a city leader and businessman in his own right. A fisherman by trade, like his father, he made his living as a wholesale fish merchant. He also spent time as a city councilman. He later married Martha "Mattie" Raulerson, and they had two daughters, Mildred and Lenora. Simeon built the family home on what is now US Highway 1. Simeon's daughter Lenora became a successful businesswoman, operating women's and children's clothing stores in both Fort Pierce and Sebastian. Mildred went to school in Jacksonville to study business and, later, nursing. She became a registered nurse and served as the superintendent of the hospitals in Fort Pierce and, later, Rockledge, Florida. She eventually returned to Sebastian, where she assisted Lenora in managing the store. Neither sister ever married, and both lived in the home their father built in Sebastian until they passed away, Mildred in 1991 and Lenora in 1995.

The house was owned by several corporations after Lenora Park's death. The structure is now part of a larger commercial area in the 1100 block of South US Highway 1 in Sebastian and is known as the District Sebastian.

The home built by Simeon Park in 1913 as it looks today in Sebastian, Florida. Park was the son of original Sebastian settler August Park. *Larry Lawson.*

The current owners, Jason and Suzanne Wille, are well aware of the rumors of ghostly activity in their historic building.

One such story involves a previous tenant who operated a hair salon in the building and reported numerous unexplained events in their business. Strange noises and voices were heard, along with a disturbing event that occurred in one of the hairstyling rooms. A cart in front of a window in the rear of the room contained a jar of hair gel. Employees of the salon observed the jar of hair gel levitate off the cart and fall to the ground.

In later years, a small coffee shop occupied the space at the south end of the building. The owner of the shop reported that an older woman with long gray hair entered the restaurant and asked for a cup of coffee. The woman then remarked that the store didn't look anything like it did when she lived there. The shop owner, intrigued by that comment, poured her the coffee and placed in on the counter. When she looked to complete the purchase, the woman was nowhere to be found in the store. It was like she had vanished. Not long after that, the owner of the complex was outside near the retention pond in the back of the building. He reported seeing an older woman by the pond, staring out into the water. When he looked again, the woman was gone. She had vanished again.

In more recent times, a realty company occupies the office once used by the hair salon. It was reported that a filing cabinet in one of the rooms in the rear of the office was constantly found with its drawers pulled open, even after office staff verified they had closed them. Employees also complained of items located on top of the cabinet being moved when nobody in the office had moved them. What makes these reports even more remarkable is that this cabinet sits in front of the same window where the jar of hair gel levitated from its cart and fell to the ground. It is also said that this was the same window Lenora Park used to sit by to stare out at the pond in the back of her home. Coincidence, or is Lenora Park sending the message that she does not like having her view of the pond blocked?

In another report, building owner Suzanne Wille told this author that an old bell attached to the interior wall of the house continues to ring on its own. There is no breeze that could reach it or any explainable reason that the bell should be heard. Maybe someone just wants the new owners to realize they are still there.

Do the Park sisters still inhabit the home they lived in for most of their lives? Are they unhappy with the current use of their home? Perhaps a chat by the pond is in order to solve this mystery.

PREACHER'S ISLAND

The Indian River, along the shores of Sebastian and Vero Beach, is lined with many small islands. Some are known as spoil islands, dots of land created by the dredging of the river in the 1940s and 1950s. There are also natural islands in the river. One of those natural islands holds a mystery that remains unresolved today.

In the Indian River, nestled between Sebastian and the unincorporated area called Wabasso, Preacher's Island was well known among the early settlers of Indian River County. Of course, it wasn't called Preacher's Island in those early days. It was just another place for clamming, relaxation and exploring. It became known as Preacher's Island after the now-infamous Reverend Thomas New, former postmaster of Newhaven (later known as Sebastian).

Reverend New, a retired Methodist pastor from the Detroit, Michigan area, came to the Sebastian area around 1880. New had plans for the area known then as St. Sebastian. He believed that an opening could be created outside of the barrier island that would lead to the river, opening up St. Sebastian to growth and prosperity. His vision was to open this passage by shovel and allow the tide to expand and deepen the cut naturally. New advertised and heavily promoted the area, hoping to attract residents and business. This spot became known as News Cut. Despite his efforts, and the help of others from the community, the project failed. The tide did just the opposite of what New expected and filled the channel in. (Eventually, in 1918, the Sebastian Inlet District created a new inlet, just north of News Cut.)

As Thomas New worked to create his subtropical paradise, he opened up a mercantile store and established a post office, naming this developing village Newhaven. He was appointed postmaster and began to build his new life. But trouble was not long in coming. In 1884, New was accused of wrongdoing by local government officials. Some say he was involved in the illegal sale of liquor or that he tampered with the mail. There were even rumors of financial improprieties. Whatever the reason, Thomas New resigned his duties as postmaster that same year. August Park became the temporary postmaster until Sylvanus Kitching was named permanent postmaster. Kitching then changed the name of the post office and town to Sebastian. But that was not to be the end of Thomas News's story. He still had more excitement to provide this tiny fishing village.

It had been rumored for several years that New had discovered some treasure in the area. Some thought it was some of the treasure lost in the sinking of the 1715 Spanish treasure fleet. Local residents had seen him going out to an island in the river south of town by himself, often in the evening. This only caused more suspicion and rumors that the Reverend New had something to hide. New, questioned about the rumors and his solitary trips to the island, continued to deny possession or knowledge of any hidden treasure.

It was early October 1885 when two boys were searching for clams in the river just north of present-day Wabasso, Florida, and spotted something unusual. The boys were in a popular location for clamming. As they searched for spots to dig up this shelled delicacy, they noticed someone on the island next to them. They recognized the person as Reverend New. The boys saw him digging on the island and believed they had actually caught him in the process of gathering the treasure he was long believed to have. The boys, knowing they now had proof of the preacher's treasure stash, hurried home and excitedly described to their parents what they had seen. The boys insisted that their parents go with them back out to the island to see it for themselves. But their parents refused, saying it could not have been the aging clergyman. The boys insisted they had recognized New and caught him in the act of digging up his treasure. The boys' parents also continued to tell them that they did not see Thomas New out on the island, that it was impossible. They explained to their sons that Reverend Thomas New was very ill and bedridden at the home of another family.

New was indeed terminally ill and died in the home of August Park on October 8, 1885, just days after the two boys believed they saw him on the island. In fact, Thomas New had been ill and unable to leave his bed for weeks prior to his death.

So, who was it that these two young fishermen saw on the island? In those early days of Sebastian, there were few permanent settlers, and most of the residents knew each other. How could the boys make such a mistake in identification? Or did they? Is it possible the Reverend New's illness was so critical that it resulted in his spirit being able to release itself and appear where he felt he needed to be? Was New, in spirit form, taking the final steps to forever conceal his secret? Whatever the reason, the belief that New did have something to hide resulted in treasure hunters searching the island for years to discover what he left behind. To this day, his secret has never been uncovered on the island that is, consequently, now known as Preacher's Island.

CHAPTER 10

POTTINGER AND SON FUNERAL HOME

T his quaint apartment building that sits on the northwest corner of Washington Street and Indian River Drive was built in 1942. In 1971, it became the location of the Daniel R. Pottinger Colonial Funeral Home. In 1980, the name of the business changed to Pottinger and Son Funeral Home as Daniel Pottinger Jr. joined the family business, which continued to serve the community as one of the oldest family-owned funeral homes in Indian River County. Daniel R. Pottinger was very active in the community. He served in many capacities with the Sebastian River Chamber of Commerce, including two terms as president of the chamber. His son Daniel Pottinger Jr. was also very active in the Sebastian Lion's and Shriner's Clubs. In late 1987, the Pottingers sold the business, and the building was transformed into an apartment building. The residents who lived there over the ensuing years began to find that perhaps others who had spent time there were not yet ready to leave.

The stories told by the residents of the apartment building are both fascinating and sad. It has been said that the spirit of a small girl still haunts the balconies and hallways of the building. She has been reported standing on either of the two second-floor balconies that face Indian River Drive on the eastern side of the building. Some say that she is crying and others that she is laughing, but all have noted that she is playing with what appears to be a rubber ball. She is seen bouncing it either on the balcony or in the hallways of dwellings. According to several reports, the ball was seen falling from the balcony and disappearing. Two former residents were so unnerved

The building that housed the Pottinger Funeral Home from 1971 until around 1987. *Larry Lawson.*

by the spectral visits that they sought out someone to investigate who it was that haunted their building.

Other than those who have already passed on, there have been no known reported deaths in the old Pottinger Funeral Home. Could it be that the little girl who's been reported there enjoys the surroundings of the old funeral home and is content to stay? Or is she stuck in this realm, looking in vain for her family? Regardless, the stories of a young child roaming the halls of the former Pottinger Funeral Home continue to tug at the heartstrings of anyone who hears them.

CHAPTER 11
THE ASHLEY GANG'S LAST STAND

Much has been written over the decades about the Ashley gang. This infamous group of bandits, bootleggers and smugglers was controlled by John Ashley and his paramour, Laura Upthegrove. They were the Treasure Coast and Indian River County's most notorious criminal gang in the early 1920s. This is almost a decade before another gang led by the infamous Bonnie Parker and Clyde Barrow—Bonnie and Clyde.

The Ashley Gang's reign of terror stretched from southern present-day Martin County, where the city of Stuart sits, to Sebastian in northern Indian River County. While the Ashleys' hideout was in the Gomez area of Martin County, they still spent considerable time in Indian River County. There is speculation that they had connections to old Fellsmere, which had a growing reputation at that time as a haven for bootleggers, poachers and other criminal types.

But it was in Sebastian that this infamous gang met its end. In February 1924, Palm Beach County sheriff Robert Baker ambushed the Ashley Gang at their hideout in Gomez. There was no attempt to capture the clan as deputies fired into the camp, injuring and killing several members of the gang, including John Ashley's elderly father, Joe Ashley. This resulted in John, in a fit of anger, killing the first deputy he saw during the gunfight. Fred Baker, the cousin of Sheriff Robert Baker, was the victim of Ashley's rage. This event led to heightened tensions and resulted in Ashley and his top three lieutenants, Ray Lynn, Clarence Middleton and Hanford Mobley, fleeing from town, taking the Old Dixie Highway up to Jacksonville. There,

Ashley was going to take care of some other business ventures. His plan was to return home in time to assassinate Sheriff Baker before the November 1924 election for sheriff.

But who did Ashley not plan on taking? His girlfriend and partner in crime Laura Upthegrove, also known as the Queen of the Everglades. Word was that she was angry about this slight from Ashley and, out of revenge, tipped off a Palm Beach County deputy about the boys' impending road trip. This deputy immediately reported the information to Sheriff Baker. Baker reached out to his colleague in St. Lucie County, Sheriff J.R. Merritt. Baker told Merritt what John Ashley was up to and went on to explain that he dared not leave Palm Beach because that would send a clear signal to the Ashley Gang that he was onto them. Baker asked Merritt if he would stop the gang, and Merritt agreed to it, though allegedly with reservations.

So, on November 1, 1924, fate finally met up with John Ashley. Sheriff Merritt had set up a ruse on the bridge on the Old Dixie Highway crossing the river into Brevard County. At this time in history, Indian River County did not exist, so Sebastian was the northernmost point in St. Lucie County. Sheriff Merritt placed a chain across the two-lane wooden bridge crossing the fork on the river and hung a lantern on it, indicating the bridge was closed. He stationed his posse—included several of his deputies, Palm Beach deputies and the Stuart police chief—in the woods surrounding the bridge entrance. Merritt also found two young men from Sebastian loitering there and told them they needed to leave. The boys said they would but instead hid nearby and watched as the cars with Ashley and his men drove up. The men stopped and got out of their automobiles to see what was wrong with the bridge. At that point, the lawmen emerged from their hiding spots and confronted the gang. The boys hiding in the woods then left and went back to Sebastian, where they spread the word of the Ashleys' capture.

What happened after that has long been up for debate, but what can't be refuted is that John Ashley, Clarence Middleton, Ray Lynn and Hanford Mobley died there in a hail of gunfire. Merritt was considered a hero by the public for stopping the Ashley menace. But he was a reluctant hero, rarely even talking about those events. He did not even use his heroic reputation for his own reelection campaign for St. Lucie County sheriff. It wasn't until over sixty years later that a few possible versions of the truth emerged publicly. There are several versions of how the gang members died. One was that Ashley made a sudden move toward a deputy, resulting in the deputy firing his gun, causing all the other deputies to fire also. Another is that Ashley simply sneezed, causing the violent reaction. Another is that law enforcement never intended to allow these criminals to be arrested only for them to potentially escape again, and thus they were executed. Whatever actually happened that night, the story ended for the Ashley Gang at the south end of that bridge.

But members of the Ashley Gang still allegedly remind the present world that they were there. For decades since that fateful night, there have been reports from residents on both sides of the river of gunshots ringing out in the middle of the night followed by moans of the dying. Perhaps the violence of their deaths has sentenced John Ashley and his companions to forever remain in the place of their demise.

PART III
FELLSMERE: A HISTORY

Fellsmere was a city built from swampland and was originally known as Cinncinnatus. It was owned by A.O. Russell, a paper manufacturer, from Cincinnati, Ohio, who was best known for the production of playing cards. It was his desire to develop this 115,000-acre parcel into the Cinncinnatus Farm Company, which he did in 1895.

Russell had built a narrow-gauge railroad to supply equipment, personnel and material to his project west of the small fishing enclave of Sebastian. By this time, Henry Flagler's Florida East Coast railroad had reached Sebastian, and Russell desired to connect his tracks to Flagler's system. Russell planned on eventually connecting his railway from the Florida East Coast Line all the way to Kissimmee, Florida, but he died in 1900 before the work could be completed. The area lay dormant for a period. Access to the area was only possible by the rail line Russell built, making it difficult for anyone to develop it further. The property sat in probate, with investors showing interest. But in March 1910, a man named Nelson Fell put down $63,125 on 118,000 acres of land, leaving a balance of $91,875 (a cost of $1.35 per acre). It was Fell's desire to develop the property, formerly known as Cinncinnatus, into a farming mecca.

Nelson Fell, a New Zealander by birth who was educated in England, was an engineer by trade. He was already familiar with Florida, as he had lived there in the late 1800s. During the first land boom in the state, Fell founded a small town near present-day Orlando named Narcoossee and sat on the town's first city council in the late 1880s. By 1895, however, unexpected freezes and stalled growth in Florida had ended this first land boom, and Nelson entered a new endeavor. Working with his brother, Arthur, in London, Nelson became part of a plan to purchase and run a copper mine in Siberia near present-day Kazakhstan. It was here that Fell made his fortune, and in 1909, he came back to the United States able to retire a wealthy man. Being the entrepreneur he was, Fell could not stay out of the business world long. He was made aware of that patch of land west of Sebastian and purchased it. Here, the next chapter in his life began.

In this swampy, mosquito-infested piece of Florida, Nelson's next adventure began to develop. The burgeoning new town became known as Fellsmere, *Fell* after the man himself and *mere*, meaning "a watery place," describing the swamp-like conditions that were natural to the land. When construction began in Fellsmere, the town was in the northernmost part of St. Lucie County, which was created out of the southern part of Brevard County in 1905. By 1915, Fellsmere had been incorporated and was the largest city in St. Lucie County after the county seat, the city of Fort Pierce. Fellsmere's incorporation as a municipality in 1915 was the culmination of many exciting things. Fellsmere became a place of growth. In 1915, it was the first municipality incorporated in what is now Indian River County. One of the most interesting historical facts about Fellsmere is that it became the birthplace of woman suffrage in the South. It was in Fellsmere, in 1915, during the first municipal elections for town leaders that a woman voted for the first time in the United States south of the Mason-Dixon line. It is said that when the St. Lucie County supervisor of elections found that a woman had voted, he attempted to void the vote, but the city refused, making this election a nationally historic event. Fellsmere went on to be the first incorporated municipality in what is now Indian River County. It was the first town in the area to have sidewalks, electricity and telephone service. It also has the boasting rights to the oldest brick-and-mortar schoolhouse in present-day Indian River County. The future looked bright for Nelson Fell's dream.

But it was in the summer of 1915, not long after the town elections, that his good fortune began to unravel. A heavy storm caused flooding in the town. The newly dredged canals that were designed to prevent flooding were not able to handle the water unleashed by the storm. Much of the town flooded, washing away the dreams and hopes of those who lived and had begun to thrive in Fellsmere. The flooding caused so much damage that in 1916, the Fellsmere Farms Company was unable to meet its payment obligations, and the company went into receivership. The future of the town appeared broken. By 1917, Fell and his family had left Fellsmere forever. Fell passed away in Warrington, Virginia, in 1928.

In 1918, a man named Frank Heiser took the reins of this faltering area and helped save it by bringing in the commodity of sugar. He built the first sugar refinery in the state of Florida in the northwestern Fellsmere area. Under Heiser's leadership, Fellsmere was able to stabilize and find its way through the Depression and the war years, ultimately making its mark in the citrus industry. While it never attained the stature that Nelson Fell had envisioned, Fellsmere survived, and it has become the beloved home of many. Today it is most commonly recognized as the home of the Frog Leg Festival. This event was created over thirty years ago by city resident, business owner and former county commissioner Fran Adams to raise money for youth athletics and recreation in the city. The festival has grown to be one of the largest public events in the county, with its focus on frog leg and alligator meals. In fact, Fellsmere is listed in the Guinness Book of World Records for the most frog leg dinners sold at one time!

The city has grown and triumphed over the obstacles thrown at it over the years. Fellsmere has become a symbol of the grit and determination it took to carve a life out of the tropical wetlands of Florida in the early part of the twentieth century.

CHAPTER 1

FELLSMERE OLD SCHOOL / CITY HALL

When the Fellsmere school opened in 1916, it was state of the art. Fellsmere was still part of St. Lucie County at that time, but the school was destined to become the first brick-and-mortar schoolhouse in what was to become Indian River County in 1925. The school was originally part of the independent Fellsmere School District and served the children in the area from elementary school all the way through high school. It was in the 1960s that the Fellsmere School converted to kindergarten through eighth grade; the children of high school age were sent to Vero Beach High School. After the school closed in 1980, the building became the town's city hall for a while but later sat derelict for an even longer period. Had it not been for herculean efforts by Fellsmere citizens to preserve this landmark, specifically a man named Clarence "Korky" Korker, this building would have been destroyed and carried away, along with its history and memories. After years of hard work, the school was remodeled and modernized and again became the home of Fellsmere city government. It stands today as a testament to the pioneers who carved a place to live and thrive out of the swamplands.

The paranormal activity at the old school/city hall has long been spoken about among the residents and employees of Fellsmere. It became a topic of discussion outside the city when a member of Fellsmere's maintenance team spoke of it openly to others. Leti Areola described how her first encounter was when she unlocked the back doors of the old schoolhouse to begin her duties inside one evening. As she was doing this, she noticed a young

The Fellsmere School. The school was opened in 1916 and was the local school until it closed in 1981. *Larry Lawson.*

boy, approximately ten to twelve years of age, sitting next to the doors. He was wearing a long-sleeved white shirt, short pants with suspenders and a newsboy-style cap, a look that might remind one of the Depression era. They looked at each other and acknowledged one another. Leti briefly looked away, thinking how unusual the situation was, and when she looked back, the young boy was gone. According to Leti, this was just the first of many encounters she had inside the building.

Leti tells stories of times her broom was grabbed as she was sweeping and finding items on desks that she moved to clean elsewhere when she finished her duties, as if they'd been moved, as well as small pebbles being tossed at her by an unseen hand. Probably the most interesting series of events she relayed was when she would clean the glass windows in the building's doors over the weekend, only to return on Monday to see children's fingerprints on the glass. This was witnessed by another city employee after Memorial Day weekend in 2016.

Leti came to work the morning after the long Memorial Day weekend and observed something that unnerved her. She clearly saw children's fingerprints on the glass window of the door leading into a room on the second floor referred to as the choir room. Leti had last cleaned that window on Friday evening, and there had been no one in the building for three days. She immediately went to the police department, summoned a police officer and led him back to the city hall. She brought the attention of the police officer to several sets of small, childlike fingerprints. Leti explained that she had cleaned those windows on Friday and no one, especially not young children, had been in the building since she cleaned. The police officer confirmed the presence of these fingerprints. This type of evidence was also confirmed by the staff of the Fellsmere's Boy's and Girl's Club, which, at that time, utilized the basement floor of the building. The director of the program had seen this herself, noticing children's fingerprints on door windows when no one had been in the building all weekend after they were cleaned.

This wasn't the only thing the program director experienced. She and other staff members have reported observing the elevator in the building moving between floors on its own when they were there in the evenings after the city hall had closed. They've also reported loud banging directly on the doors of the elevator when no one was in there. The city had the elevators checked by an engineer, who was unable to identify a mechanical reason for the elevator to move on its own or make those banging sounds. The staff went on to describe how young children who attended the club told them of seeing other little children they had spoken and interacted with who were not seen by anyone else.

Members of the Fellsmere City Police Department also continued to have encounters with the other side. A former officer reported that he clearly recalled an episode from the rear parking lot of the police station. He stated that when he was standing in the back lot of the police department at about three o'clock one morning, he saw something that made his blood run cold. The school was still undergoing renovation at the time, and he was looking up at the building into the windows where the city manager's office would eventually be located. He stated that he clearly saw an individual standing in the window looking back at him. From that time forward, the officer refused to enter that building at night alone.

In another incident, the Fellsmere chief of police, Keith Touchberry, returned to the police station after a meeting in the city hall building and asked the detective on duty (this author), to immediately check the meeting room on the second floor of the city hall/old school. He stated that during the meeting with several other community leaders, a door leading to another room suddenly opened and shut on its own, in full view of everyone in attendance. The detective carefully checked the door and the floor to see if there was a natural or man-made explanation for what happened. There was not.

The city clerk later told the author of another incident when she stayed working late one night in the city hall. She was in the building by herself when she heard the bloodcurdling scream of a man coming from the attic area of the building, just outside her office. The opening to the attic was closed and required a ladder to enter. The attic trapdoor was shut, and there was no ladder present. The city clerk elected not to work late by herself ever again.

Another member of the city government informed the author that he once saw a young boy sitting on the bench outside of what is now the city's Water and Building Department. He said that the boy was sitting there with his head down, moving his legs back and forth under the bench. He looked as if he was waiting to be scolded. This office was where the school principal's office would have been during the days when the building was the Fellsmere School. This city official gave a familiar description of a boy about ten to twelve years of age wearing a long-sleeved white shirt, short pants with suspenders and a newsboy-style cap. This was the same description provided by Leti in her earlier encounter.

This spirit has become known as Billy. Billy is one of the many spirits of students that are said to continue to inhabit this building. Children running and laughing in the halls have been heard by numerous city employees and visitors. On one occasion, the voice of Billy appears to have been captured. Mark Holt, paranormal investigator and member of the Indian River Historical Society, was in the auditorium of the school with other members of a paranormal team. While in the auditorium, he was using a digital voice recorder. He asked if that was the room Billy liked to be in. When Mark and the group played the recorder back, they heard a very clear child's voice simply say, "Yes sir."

The stories and experiences of those who have felt or witnessed paranormal events in Fellsmere's city hall/old school are well documented. As research continues there, hopefully some answers will be found about why these young students continue to stay. There are no records of any tragedies in the building, which are often associated with spirits being trapped in a location. In fact, there are few records from the early years of the school. Originally, Fellsmere was its own school district, keeping its own records. Very few of those records exist today. This lack of information came to light while the city was preparing for the one hundredth anniversary of the school in 2016. Organizers of the anniversary celebration were unable to locate many past students to invite because there are no attendance records from those early days.

From the sounds of children running in the halls late at night to fingerprints appearing on cleaned windows and city staff and administrators witnessing unexplained events, is there any doubt of the paranormal activity in the Fellsmere old school/city hall? Those who live and work in the city certainly don't think so.

CHAPTER 2

MARSH LANDING RESTAURANT

What's now the Marsh Landing Restaurant was the original home of the Fellsmere Estates Corporation, the company that was to entice northerners to come to Fellsmere and enjoy what the subtropical climate had to offer. Unfortunately, when the offices for the Fellsmere Estates Corporation were built in 1925, the country was beginning to feel the effects of the coming economic depression, and what was known as the Third Florida Land Boom came to a crashing halt. Nelson Fell had left the town bearing his name in 1917. A man named Frank Heiser now held the reins of Fellsmere's future. When the Fellsmere Estates Corporation failed, this stately building was left unoccupied. Not too long after that, it became the headquarters of the Florida Sugar Corporation, which would see Fellsmere through the Great Depression all the way to the early 1960s. The town became known for the production of sugar. A little-known fact is that in the early 1930s, Fellsmere became the home of the first sugar refinery in Florida, a plant perched on the western edge of town.

Sugar was king in Fellsmere until the 1960s. This new era brought much change, as sugar gave way to massive citrus groves. The railway that had served Fellsmere no longer existed, and the town began to set its sights on the future. This future no longer seemed to include the iconic building that still held the name of its first owner, the Fellsmere Estates Corporation, emblazed across the front. It was used for city hall and the police department for a time and finally found itself abandoned and empty. Eventually, it was

The Marsh Landing Restaurant. Originally home of the Fellsmere Estates Corporation, it was constructed in 1925. After restoration, it became the Marsh Landing Restaurant. *Larry Lawson.*

used once a year by the Sebastian Women's Club for their regionally known haunted house during the Halloween season. How ironic that is.

In 1995, the building was purchased by Fran Adams, a local resident and former Indian River County commissioner. Adams understood the importance of preserving the history of Fellsmere and fought to ensure that the past would be remembered. She led this fight by purchasing the old Fellsmere Estates Corporation building and developing it into the renowned Marsh Landing Restaurant, recognized throughout the state of Florida for its old Florida cuisine. As the remodeling began, something was awakened that no one, especially Fran Adams, expected. Unexplained noises and movements were noticed as construction went on, though not enough to cause a delay in the opening of this new business. The activity became more noticeable after the opening of the restaurant, almost as if the former inhabitants were coming forth to see the new surroundings. Whether they approve or disapprove of the changes remains to be seen.

The restaurant had a reputation for being haunted—a reputation never denied by owner Fran Adams or her staff. When you meet Fran for the first time, it is immediately apparent that she is a no-nonsense businessperson who gets straight to the point. When asked if paranormal activity occurs in her restaurant, she laughs and asks which events you want to know about. She will then proceed to tell you about the most common visitor from the other side, the lady in white. Fran describes the apparition as a woman wearing a white dress floating from the west side of the main dining room to the east.

Fran explains that the woman does not appear to notice anyone or react to anything in this realm. She just stares straight ahead and moves from one point to another. This incident has occurred at least half a dozen times in the exact same way, as if it was a video recording being played over and over again. Fran feels as though it is the daughter of Nelson Fell, Marian, that she has seen. However, history reports that the Fell family left in 1917, and the building was constructed in 1925. So who was the ghostly visitor? Could it have been another woman whose energy was trapped in the old wood that was used to build the original Florida Estates Corporation? Or was it Marian Fell, whose energy was absorbed by the land on which the restaurant now resides?

Fran also describes seeing another woman wearing a gray sweater in what is now the banquet room of the restaurant. She speaks of seeing strange orbs of light on the building's surveillance cameras, the restaurant radio going on and off by itself and the restaurant's cash registers sometimes acting as if they had a mind of their own by ringing up unseen customers. Other restaurant workers corroborate these experiences. The events manager for the restaurant, Amber Cerda, explained that years ago, when she was the night manager, she was completing the locking of the building one night when she heard a loud crash coming from the office. On investigating the sound, she found that the cabinet inside the office that had all the keys hanging in it was, strangely, standing open. She then noticed that the keys were no longer hanging on the cabinet door but were strewn all over the office floor.

Another former night manager, Casey Spivey, described to the author something that happened to her as she was locking up one night. She stated that she was beginning her final check and was walking from the office to the south side of the building where the restrooms are located when she passed by a round table and found one of the chairs, which were normally placed upside down on the tables as the floors were cleaned, was still on the floor. Casey assumed that one of the staff had simply forgotten to put the chair up, so Casey did. After checking the restroom area, she walked back by the table only to find that same chair back down and pushed into the table. Casey related to me that she just figured the permanent residents were being active again, so she put the chair back up on the table a second time. When Casey finished her closing routine, she went back out to the main floor and saw that the same chair was back down off the table and pushed in again. She decided that the chair was where they wanted it to be and left it in place.

I spoke to several current and former employees of the Marsh Landing Restaurant, and most were able to recount stories of things they have encountered. At least one employee, server Kate Daniel, reported seeing Nelson Fell himself in the building. Employees also speak of finding mounted deer heads in the banquet room on the floor when they opened up in the morning. The deer heads in question have a mount with a slotted hole for a peg, large and rounded at the bottom of the slot and narrow on the top. This allows for the mount to be placed over the flattened head of the peg and moved down to secure the piece to the wall. In other words, the peg is securely anchored to the wall. The deer mounts were found on the floor, base down with no damage. The pegs remained securely attached to the wall. The pegs were not torn from the wall, which meant that the mount had to be lifted up on the peg and removed through the wide part of the slot on the mount before it could come off the wall. The author was on duty with the police department when called over to the restaurant early one morning as the staff opened up and observed a deer mount on the floor. If it had fallen off on its own, the peg would have been torn from the wall and the mount most assuredly would have struck the table beneath it, probably damaging it. Yet there was no damage.

Another piece of memorabilia that mysteriously fell from its mounting was an antique child's toy tractor. This tractor was a pedal toy that a young child could ride. When the restaurant opened, it was mounted on a ledge along with other antiques. That tractor sat there for over twenty years with no movement. Years after it was placed there, security cameras filmed the tractor mysteriously coming off the ledge, its pedal digging a hole into the floor. There was no indication of the tractor coming loose or faltering in its placement. Nothing else on the ledge showed any movement at all. What caused this sudden movement? Just one more mystery attached to the Marsh Landing Restaurant.

Guests from all over the Treasure Coast and the state of Florida have come to the Marsh Landing Restaurant with the hopes of experiencing something otherworldly. But it was in May 2016 that one of the most astonishing experiences there occurred. Misty Simpson, a guest at a public investigation being held at the restaurant, took two photographs of the area in the main dining room facing the women's restroom. The photographs were taken two seconds apart. The first showed the area with the women's restroom, door propped open, complete with a chair rail visible on the wall inside the room. The second photograph, taken two seconds later, shows a figure with a large hat and dark purple–appearing garment, possibly a dress, standing in the doorway of the women's restroom; the chair rail is clearly seen through the figure's chest. Shocked at what her cellphone captured on its camera, Misty quickly informed event staff. According to Misty and event staff, there was no one in the bathroom at the time. A surveillance camera was pointed in that direction, clearly showing the restroom. The camera did not record the presence of anyone, guest or staff member, in the area of the restroom at that time. It also did not reveal anyone wearing the garments seen in the photograph. Attempts were immediately undertaken to recreate the event to see if there was a logical explanation. None was found. Had Misty Simpson photographed a visitor from the other side?

An examination of the cell phone that took the photograph as well as the photograph itself was completed in a forensic laboratory. While the examiner would not say the photograph was of an apparition, they did say that the cell phone did take the photographs two seconds apart and there were no digital applications, overlays or anything else altering the picture. The photograph was determined to be authentic and has become known as Marsh Landing's Lady in Purple.

It seems as though the women's restroom is a particularly active area. Restaurant staff are fearful of going in there when opening or closing due to the shadows that whisk by them. On one occasion, guests observed a cat in the room that suddenly disappeared. It appears you are never alone when you use the ladies' restroom at the Marsh Landing.

There is a room off the main dining area to the west that is suitable for small groups to enjoy their meals. It is called the Frog Room for its décor honoring the many years the city has hosted the Frog Leg Festival. The Frog Room was one of the first places where evidence of paranormal activity was detected during investigations of the building. While activity is often detected with various EMF instruments, in this case, it was the answers received using dowsing rods and recorded EVPs that indicated the room appeared to be occupied by two older ladies from the past. These otherworldly visitors tended to complain about the man in the bar whom they disliked. The same equipment revealed a tall older gentleman in the room to the north of the main dining room, known as the bar. This does not mean the visitors stay in these rooms, however, as one investigator caught a clear EVP in the Frog Room of a deep male voice saying, "I'm

Photo of the famous "Lady in Purple" ghost taken by Misty Simpson inside the Marsh Landing Restaurant in 2016. *Misty Simpson.*

the guy in the bar!" It was believed this was the same man that the ladies in the Frog Room grumbled about.

But others there also want their presence to be recognized. During another event, the building was secured in order to begin. One of the first orders of business was closing the restaurant's window blinds. As the investigators emerged from the banquet room after a pre-investigation briefing, they found, to their surprise, one set of blinds open again. It was later revealed by restaurant staff that a former patron often sat near the window where the blinds had mysteriously reopened. This patron preferred to have the blinds open so he could see outside. He had died recently. It appeared as if he was still enjoying his coffee at the restaurant from the other side.

The kitchen of the Marsh Landing is not immune to paranormal activity, either. In October 2019, the author observed the figure of a tall, lanky male appearing in the hallway leading to the kitchen area and disappearing into the wall. The figure left a strong impression of a cattleman or cowboy. Another investigator reported seeing a shadow in that same spot, crossing the hall, on another visit there. Restaurant staff have also reported seeing dishes stacked up in the food prep area in the kitchen move on their own

With all the evidence piling up, the Marsh Landing Restaurant continues to have a story to tell.

CHAPTER 3

MARIAN FELL LIBRARY

As Nelson Fell directed the growth of this young municipality, it was his daughter, Marian, who looked to develop a legacy of culture in Fellsmere. Marian Fell wanted the town to have its own library and convinced her father of the need. Fell heard his daughter's request and said he would build her this library, but she would be responsible for financing it. Marian agreed to the conditions and developed her plan to finance the building in a unique way. During her family's time in Russia, Marian had learned much about Russian language and culture. Through her contacts there, she was able to gain permission to translate the writings of great Russian authors, such as Chekov, into the English language and then sold these translations. The money gained from that endeavor allowed her to pay her father in order to build this small library on Cypress Street on the north side of town. The library opened in 1914 as one of the centerpieces of this new community.

The Marian Fell Library stands today in its original location. The building, while modified somewhat to comply with modern code, looks much the same as it did in 1914. It is still operational and is therefore the oldest operating library in what is now Indian River County.

Rumors have swirled around the community for years about unusual activity inside the library: the sounds of footsteps from an unseen person, sudden drops in temperature and voices have all been reported. But perhaps it is the events that have occurred while guests to the city were touring this remarkable building over the years that have kept people talking.

Marian Fell Library in Fellsmere, Florida. Opened in 1914, it is the oldest operating library in Indian River County. *Larry Lawson.*

During these tours, guests reported the feeling of being watched, and on one specific occasion, they saw a broom cover in the restroom move on its own. This broom cover, designed to look like a doll, allegedly turned on its own and was witnessed by a guest. To this day, it is said that the library staff will not touch the doll-shaped broom cover.

During another tour, one of the chairs placed on top of a small child's table fell on its own. This event was witnessed by several people and left them considerably shaken. The chairs had been placed seat down on top of the table with their legs interlocking. The witnesses saw one of the chairs slide off the table and come crashing to the floor without disturbing any other chair on the table. This feat appeared impossible, considering all the chairs had their legs interlocked with the others. Tour company staff were called to the scene after the occurrence and observed the table with the chairs sitting on it and the single chair lying on the floor. An attempt to recreate the event and debunk what had happened was unsuccessful, leaving all who had witnessed it wondering what they had just experienced. All the chairs were placed on the table in such a way that if any moved, it had to hit the adjoining one, causing a domino effect of movement. The only way one chair could have been knocked off the table and landed on the floor would have been for it to be lifted straight up and then dropped straight down. Based on the physical nature of the event as well as eyewitness accounts, there was no normal explanation for what occurred. Perhaps a paranormal explanation was the answer.

Individuals with the ability to see through the veil of this dimension into the next have reported that the building is still watched over by librarians of the past. Perhaps they have had enough of visitors coming through their library making too much noise and have decided to let them know that they are unhappy with their conduct.

CHAPTER 4

SECTION FOREMAN'S HOUSE

The Section Foreman's House is one of the oldest structures in the city of Fellsmere. Built around 1911 on the tracks of the old Fellsmere Railroad, it served as the quarters for train and railway crews traveling back and forth along the line. It sat on the same location for over one hundred years until it was moved approximately a quarter mile to the west to be part of a new recreational area envisioned by the city of Fellsmere. Prior to its being moved, it had been a private residence and then sat abandoned for several years.

Shortly before it was moved, a paranormal team was able to conduct the only investigation of the property. Not much information was revealed by the building, but that didn't mean there wasn't someone watching. One member of this team, Evan Lawson, reported that he observed people outside the building. Staring into the woods, he looked mesmerized. When asked what it was, what he was looking at, all he could say was, "They're watching us." When asked who he saw, he could only say, "The Indians."

In the time before settlers came to the area and before the Europeans discovered Florida, the Ais culture had a very strong presence in this area. Some of their mounds, or middens, found around Fellsmere contain the remains of tribe members or articles of their life. Several still dot the area at protected locations. When Evan had this experience of being watched, he said that he felt they were merely watching to make sure no one did anything wrong to the land or showed disrespect to it.

Shortly thereafter, the building was moved to its current location and refurbished, and the author visited the area with another curious individual. It was in the middle of a typical hot Florida summer day. The temperature was in the low to mid-ninety-degree range with the humidity over 90 percent. Standing in what was the backyard of the house, the author held a device that monitored temperature and electromagnetic fields. It was at that time that both individuals felt the area suddenly become cooler, and the device recorded a sudden fifteen-degree drop in temperature. The electromagnetic field (EMF) detector fully activated, indicating an electrical source was nearby. As suddenly as this event happened, it stopped. There was no significant breeze or any other logical explanation for the sudden drop in temperature and nothing that should have caused the EMF meter to react.

Could this have been a classic example of the land, not a building, being haunted? Were the same members of the Ais people seen during the earlier investigation there to remind us of who protects this land? Were they wanting to make sure that we showed the appropriate reverence?

Never forget that it is not just structures that can be affected by paranormal forces. The land also holds the energy of those who have passed before us.

CHAPTER 5

THE FELLSMERE INN

The Fellsmere Inn was built between 1910 and 1911. It was the first building constructed by the Fellsmere Farms Company. It was designed to provide general lodging and was the primary hotel housing those who came to Fellsmere looking to purchase land. Not far from this location to the east, on what is now known as New York Avenue, sat the demonstration farms that were built to show the farming potential of the area. Those coming to see the land and make their decision about purchasing property were provided all the luxuries this tropical land could offer. The hotel was completed in March 1911 but has undergone several changes and updates through the years.

Inside, this building is a vision of the past that is enhanced with many of the modern amenities that make life in the steamy South comfortable today. One thing that has never changed, however, is what the building was constructed of: Dade County pine. This original pine found throughout the south of Florida was so hard and embedded with resin that it is almost indestructible. Many old homes and buildings that used this wood still stand today in almost the same condition as when they were built, surviving everything from termites to hurricanes. The inn's restoration was completed in 2011, and it is now a private residence. The former Fellsmere Inn is a testament to early Florida building construction and modern comfort.

But it is not just the old pine that keeps this artifact of early Fellsmere alive—it is also its past residents and guests. Over the years, the inn has been everything from a hotel to a restaurant, an antique store and someone's

The Fellsmere Inn. Constructed around 1911 by the Fellsmere Farms Corporation, it later became a restaurant, then an antique store; it is now a private residence. *Larry Lawson.*

home. Many residents of the city speak of being in the building while it was an antique store and the eerie experiences they had while inside. They claim to have heard voices and seen shadows and items moving on their own. Recent visitors have reported the presence of someone, or something, that claims to have an affinity for whiskey. Could energy from the past be trapped in the old pinewood used to build the Fellsmere Inn?

Things may go bump in the night at the old Fellsmere Inn, but what they are, or who they are, still waits to be discovered. One thing will always remain: this old hotel is a treasure of the past that continues to tell its story. Perhaps it continues to tell its story so that the future doesn't forget where Fellsmere came from.

CHAPTER 6
COUNTY ROAD 512

The road that was to become the Fellsmere Road was little more than a game trail in early years. As Fellsmere began to develop, the Fellsmere Road started as an old dirt (then shell-packed) road that took travelers from Fellsmere all the way to Sebastian. In later years, it became paved and was redesignated County Road 512 (CR512), which runs east to west linking the eastern and western parts of Indian River County. It is now one of only two roads coming in and out of Fellsmere.

Traveling west on CR512 out of Sebastian, you intersect with the overpass of Interstate 95. From there, the road darkens as you travel the last couple of miles to Fellsmere. CR512 has very little lighting west of I-95, leaving you with the feeling that you are driving into oblivion. After you pass through Fellsmere and exit to the west, you drive toward the marshes and the citrus groves that dominate that part of the county. It again becomes dark and ominous. It is on these sections of CR512 that drivers entering or leaving Fellsmere have reported the sight of a lone woman walking along the road, looking sad and forlorn. Drivers have reported seeing the woman, wearing light-colored clothing, and stopping to see if they can help, only to find that she is, inexplicably, gone.

There are no reports of a woman dying while walking along the darkened stretches of County Road 512, but there was a time, years ago, when perhaps tragedies such as that may not have been reported. So, who could the lonely lady of County Road 512 be? Perhaps, one day, she may identify herself to one of the Good Samaritans driving down that stretch of road who stop to help her. Maybe then she could provide a clue about why she inhabits the road that leads to Fellsmere.

CONCLUSION

The history of Indian River County is as complex as it is intriguing. This area was so new and unexplored for a country that was just preparing to enter the twentieth century; Florida was truly still a vast, untapped frontier. Pioneers here were experiencing hardships that settlers in the far West had left behind years before. In 1880, no roads or railroads reached what is now Indian River County. The only option to find your way to the area was via the shallow Indian River. The early settlers were forced to face tropical hardships that few in this fledgling country had to endure. They were hardy of soul and spirit and turned this area into a paradise that, years later, people would come from all over to visit or settle down for life. It was a tough, unforgiving land, but those who chose to settle it survived and thrived. Indian River County was home to a wide array of individuals, from outlaws and heroes to pirates and patriots, yet all have a place in the history shared here.

But did many of those who made their mark on Indian River County stay after they died? Does Waldo Sexton still oversee his resort? Do those who perished on these beaches still reach out to be saved? Does the Ashley Gang want to make sure they are never forgotten? That is for the reader, and those who search for those answers, to decide. But it must be said: those who have been lucky enough to experience and witness flashes of the past here in Indian River County will undoubtedly attest to the reality of paranormal existence.

GLOSSARY

DOWSING RODS: These are devices made of different materials that were originally used to find water or energy sources. Dowsing rods are a common tool used in paranormal investigations. While they have traditionally been used to find water, it is also recognized that the energy exerted by spirits is used to move them and answer simple yes or no questions. Different techniques can also be employed to find out the age, name or location of the entity communicating with the investigator. Examples of this could be: "Does your name begin with an *A*?" or "Can you point the rods to where you are standing?" While the scientific answer as to how this happens is still undiscovered, when used with other pieces of equipment and historical research, the results can remarkably accurate.

EMF (ELECTROMAGNETIC FIELD): This is a field of energy that is produced either naturally or by humans. The theory is that when spirits manifest themselves, they emit this energy and can be detected by an EMF-detecting device. EMF is also produced by electronic devices and power lines.

EVP (ELECTRONIC VOICE PHENOMENON): This is a theory regarding voices that are captured on recording devices (both digital and magnetic tape devices) but are not heard by the researcher.

SLS (STRUCTURED LIGHT SENSOR) CAMERA: A camera and projector that projects infrared dots in a grid. The sensor on the camera is able to detect and calculate items and build a three-dimensional figure or model. This camera is used for games played on a screen or TV monitor, such as games where people play tennis or another sport with an avatar seen on the screen. The avatar mimics the movements of the player so that it appears they are actually playing on the screen. The actual form of the player is represented as stick figure, and the commercial game places a figure or avatar onto the stick figure. It was found that the camera would also pick up stick figures of persons who were not there. This resulted in its evolution as a paranormal tool.

Spirit/ghost box: Also sometimes referred as a Frank's Box in honor of its creator, Frank Sumption, this device, in theory, scans radio frequencies quickly in order to detect voices from the dead. It is part of the theory known as instrumental transcommunication, which covers electronic, recording and radio devices receiving voice transmissions from the dead.

BIBLIOGRAPHY

Korker, Clarence F., and Richard B. Votapka. *A Photographic History of the City of Fellsmere*. Privately published, 2011.

Mesmer, Patrick S., and Patricia A. Mesmer. *Ghosts of the Treasure Coast*. Charleston, SC: The History Press, 2017.

Rushworth, Teresa L. *Vero Beach*. Images of America series. Charleston, SC: Arcadia Publishing, 2014.

Sebastian River Area Historical Society. *More Tales of Sebastian*. Sebastian, FL: Sebastian River Area Historical Society, 1992.

———. *Tales of Sebastian*. Sebastian, FL: Sebastian River Area Historical Society, 1990.

Sexton, Sean. *Waldo's Mountain*. Orlando, FL: Waterview Press, 2002.

Stanley, Ellen E. *Indian River County*. Images of America series. Charleston, SC: Arcadia Publishing, 2010.

———. *Pioneering Sebastian and Roseland*. Charleston, SC: Arcadia Publishing, 2017.

ABOUT THE AUTHOR

L awrence "Larry" Lawson spent over forty years in law enforcement and criminal justice education. During this time, he served as a patrol officer, detective, detective supervisor and criminal justice educator, including time as director of the Criminal Justice Institute/Police Academy for Region 11 of the State of Florida, located at Indian River State College in Fort Pierce, Florida. He holds a bachelor of science degree from Nova Southeastern University and a master's degree in public administration from Troy State University. He serves on the board of directors of the Indian River County Historical Society and is director of the Florida Bureau of Paranormal Investigation and owner of Indian River Hauntings LLC, which provides historical and paranormal tours and events. Larry has been actively researching the history and paranormal legends of the Treasure Coast of Florida since 2010.

Larry is currently the host of the radio and TV show *Paranormal Stakeout* on the X-Zone Radio and Television Broadcast Network and past host of the radio show *Encounters with the Other Side* on WPSL Radio in Fort Pierce, Florida.

You can find Larry online at https://www.indianriverhauntings.com and on Facebook.

FREE eBOOK OFFER

Scan the QR code below, enter your e-mail address and get our original Haunted America compilation eBook delivered straight to your inbox for free.

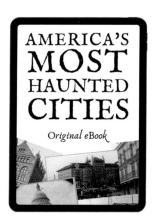

ABOUT THE BOOK

Every city, town, parish, community and school has their own paranormal history. Whether they are spirits caught in the Bardo, ancestors checking on their descendants, restless souls sending a message or simply spectral troublemakers, ghosts have been part of the human tradition from the beginning of time.

In this book, we feature a collection of stories from five of America's most haunted cities: Baltimore, Chicago, Galveston, New Orleans and Washington, D.C.

SCAN TO GET
AMERICA'S MOST HAUNTED CITIES

Having trouble scanning? Go to:
biz.arcadiapublishing.com/americas-most-haunted-cities